Illustrations by Claudio Muñoz

LIFE'S TOO
SHORT
TO
DRINK
BAD
WINE

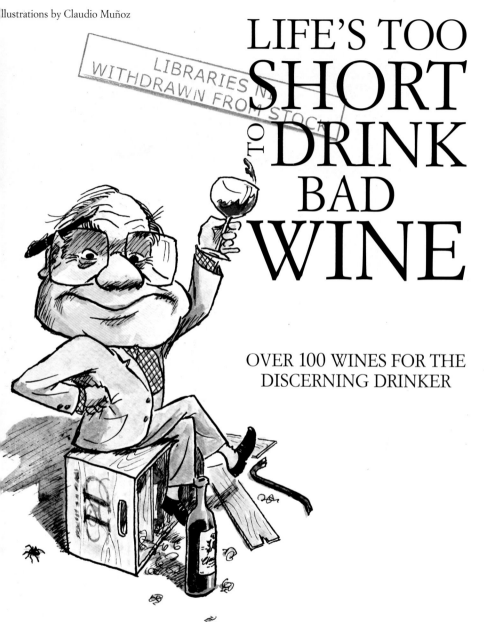

OVER 100 WINES FOR THE
DISCERNING DRINKER

SIMON HOGGART

REVISED AND UPDATED BY JONATHAN RAY

quadrille

Contents

Please note:
Top-ten wines (see page 13) are in **bold** type.
Wines are arranged in alphabetical order, and when a wine name consists of a first name and surname, the order is dictated by the surname. The denominations 'château', 'domaine (de)' and 'quinta de' are ignored for the purposes of alphabetization.

It's impossible to give hard and fast prices. These can vary enormously from merchant to merchant, and from vintage to vintage. I've used symbols to indicate the sort of price you can expect to pay. ✪ = up to £10, the kind of wine you can afford for everyday drinking. ✪✪ is £10 and over, maybe wines for a dinner party or a night in with a special meal. ✪✪✪ is about the £20 mark, a bit of a treat. Then we soar towards the pricey end, so ✪✪✪✪ would include wines at £40, the kind you might enjoy very occasionally. There are only a handful of ✪✪✪✪✪ wines – they are for daughters' weddings, 25th anniversaries, life's greatest milestones. These are the wines you might try once or twice in your whole life, but which will leave happy memories behind. Life, as the title says, is too short to drink bad wine. It is also long enough to enjoy, just sometimes, the very finest.

FOREWORD
by Jonathan Ray

I've always loved this book. It's opinionated, witty, breezy and crammed with delicious anecdotes and equally delicious wines not to mention some pretty smart tips. Simon Hoggart's zest for his subject is nothing if not infectious and there's not one bottle mentioned within these pages that I don't want to drink. In fact I'd happily open any one of them right now if you've got a corkscrew and a couple of glasses handy.

It's a perfect bedside book. It sits proudly next to other indispensable, uplifting, dip-into volumes such as Keith Waterhouse's exquisite *The Theory and Practice of Lunch* and Quentin Letts's hilarious and all-but-libellous *50 People Who Buggered Up Britain*.

When it came to wine, Simon Hoggart liked to portray himself as an enthusiastic amateur although, having seen him in action at several tastings and wine trade lunches, I knew that he knew much more than he let on. He never tired of learning more, be it by going to another tasting, by visiting another winery or simply by opening another bottle. And he was as interested in the people who made the wine as he was in the wine itself.

I first met Simon decades ago when I was in my early twenties and had no idea what I wanted to do with my life. Now in my middle fifties, sadly, I still don't. But back then there was still a chance I might end up doing something constructive and my despairing father was anxious for me to stir my stumps. As a result, he arranged a number of lunches with understanding friends and colleagues in the hope that they might light some spark of interest within me or show me a path I could follow.

One person whose good nature was thus trespassed upon was Simon Hoggart, a *Guardian* man like my father had once been and – at that time – a fellow columnist of his on *Punch* magazine, RIP. The three of us had a fine, shirt-popping lunch in London during which Simon entertained us with scurrilous stories of the Westminster village, glancing constantly this way and that at the other diners, as if distracted somehow or absorbing new material, a slight smile on his lips. He also got well stuck into the vino, something which impressed my father hugely. "An awfully fine chap, Hoggart," he declared afterwards. "I like a man who likes his wine."

Nothing came of that lunch, nor of any of the others, except a touch of indigestion, a mild hangover and a couple of slanderous stories about Alan Clark MP, a neighbour of ours and a notorious imbiber and shagger-about-town.

Strangely enough I did end up as a journalist of sorts, by chance rather than by design, although I certainly wouldn't have guessed then that a third of a century later I would have followed in Simon's impossible-to-fill shoes as drinks editor of the *Spectator*, nor indeed be revising this delightful volume. Perhaps something came of that lunch after all.

Not that *Life's Too Short to Drink Bad Wine* needed any revising. What Simon originally wrote still stands today. His advice is impeccable, be it on how to buy wine or on how to deal with sommeliers, and his tone pitch perfect. And, as I say, the 100 wines he chose are absolutely spot on, albeit that many of them are sadly outside my price range.

In fact, my only quibble is Simon's frequent bashing of Cloudy Bay in these pages. He seems to have it in for them and I think he's a little unfair. Cloudy Bay put New Zealand on the wine map and, yes, so it's owned by the vast LVMH conglomerate and, yes, it's a bit pricey compared to similar wines. And, yes, so former head winemaker Kevin Judd left to work on his own project – the excellent Greywacke – but current head winemaker Tim Heath is a worthy successor and Cloudy Bay's wines are in very fine shape. In particular, I'd urge you to give their Te Koko a try. It's certainly not cheap, but it's a cracker – a wild-fermented, oak-aged Sauvignon Blanc of immense panache. It's only ever released after three years' bottle ageing, is full of rich, rounded fresh and dried fruit, honeysuckle, herbs, nuts and cream and is unlike any other Kiwi Savvy Blanc I can think of.

But although I love it, I haven't included it in the dozen wines I've had the brass neck to add to Simon's original selection. Not because I don't rate it highly but because I've chosen another wine from New Zealand which I rate even more highly: Seresin Estate 'Leah' Pinot Noir.

Like the other eleven wines, Seresin Estate chose itself. It took me all of two minutes to compile my list. Excepting one or two absolute favourites of mine that Simon had already chosen – Pol Roger for one, Zind-Humbrecht for another – these are the wines I would hope to find bobbing beside me as I landed on my desert island.

They include two sparklers, five whites, three reds, one sweet wine and one fortified. Perfect for a series of island suppers with Girl Friday. And, quite by chance, six are from the New World (if you include England as such) and six from the Old World. A nice balance.

I like to think that Simon would have enjoyed them too and would have approved. I admired him greatly. I loved his parliamentary sketches and constantly followed his advice on wine. I just wish that he was the one revising this book and not me. Here's to you Simon.

Jonathan Ray
Brighton 2016

 Throughout the book, wine features bearing this symbol are new additions by Jonathan Ray.

INTRODUCTION

FIRST things first. These are not the top finest wines in the world. Very few of us could afford those.

Last time I looked, the 1990 Château Le Pin cost £3,800. Per bottle! The same vintage of Château Pétrus was £3,600. I know they say every single grape that goes into Le Pin is personally inspected by the *vigneron*, but even so, these prices are ludicrous. Only very rich and very vulgar people can afford them. (A friend who had been staying in one of the posher ski resorts of France reported that the place was full of Russian millionaires drinking Pétrus, and to add a bit of *whoomph* were adding slugs of vodka to the decanters. This is wine for swanking, not for drinking.)

Instead I have chosen 100 wines which are, in their entirely different ways and at their entirely different prices, delicious. They are wines that made me happy. Not wines that necessarily made me drunk, though, of course, in sufficient quantity they could do that, too. But I have always believed that you can detect wines that are made from love, as opposed to those that

are made to turn a profit. You can do both at the same time – what winemaker wants to make a loss? – but you cannot fake the dedication, the care and the character. I have chosen these because they all seem to me to have that indefinable quality, the distinction that makes them stand out from the pack. A corporate money-spinner asks how he can squeeze more product out of the crop at a lower price. A true winemaker asks how he can improve every sip – and if it costs a little bit more, so be it.

And wine is meant to cheer you up. You can guzzle beer to make you drunk; you can knock back half a bottle of whisky when the one true love of your life says goodbye. But wine is the original elixir of happiness. Is there anything that bucks you up more than a glass of cold champagne before lunch, or after work?

And the wine you drink with a meal can transform the most ordinary food into a feast. Decades ago I went out with an air stewardess who was promoted to Concorde. I knew, as it rumbled overhead, that she would be home in 40 minutes. After 20 I went to the chippie to get haddock and chips for our supper. When she arrived home clutching leftover Meursault or a superb claret, we had some of the most memorable meals that I can remember.

Wine is, naturally, a matter of personal taste. People sometimes say they are content with the mass-produced wines sold in supermarkets: Jacob's Creek, Blossom Hill, Le Piat d'Or, or Mateus Rosé. And if you are satisfied with those, you'll save a lot of money. But I suspect that most people, if asked to compare even a basic white Burgundy with Jacob's Creek Chardonnay or a New Zealand Sauvignon Blanc from its Blossom Hill equivalent, or almost any decent small-château claret from Mouton-Cadet, will not only tell the difference but prefer the former.

I recall going to a tasting of German wines with a colleague. He tried the first – from Saxony, I think – swirled it round his mouth, sucked air through his teeth in the approved fashion, then spat it out. 'Delicious!' he exclaimed. 'But I don't think I'd want to swallow it.'

There are some wines we consume in great quantities while we are students. Then we graduate and think, 'Fine, I've got a job.

I'm not on a grant any more, and I don't have to drink that stuff ever again.' The nice thing is that good wine is enjoyable even if you drink it after better wine. If you have a rich uncle who serves you Montrachet, you can still relish a Margaret River Chardonnay, made from the same grape variety in Western Australia at a fraction of the price. I doubt, however, that you'll then want to go back to Blue Nun.

The wine snob is a popular figure of caricature (remember Thurber's host saying, 'It's a naïve domestic Burgundy without any breeding, but I think you'll be amused by its presumption.') I've met a lot of wine-lovers, but very few snobs.

I suppose a snob is someone who puts more store by a name or a label than he does by the stuff in the bottle. A snob looks down his nose at a wine that comes from an area he hasn't heard of, or that didn't cost enough, or was bought in a supermarket. An enthusiast is always on the lookout for something wonderful – and if it comes from Eastern Europe, or a part of France nobody has quite heard of, or Asda, and if it costs a decent price, he is thrilled.

Mind you, there are some quite inventive snobs around. I recall going to a tasting of German wines with a colleague. He tried the first – from Saxony, I think – swirled it round his mouth, sucked air through his teeth in the approved fashion, then spat it out. 'Delicious!' he exclaimed. 'But I don't think I'd want to swallow it.' To my amazement, everyone else present, instead of bursting out in laughter, said, 'Yerrrs. We see what you mean.'

This is not to say that you should subscribe to the 'I'll drink anything provided it's alcoholic and doesn't taste as if it's meant to unblock drains' school of wine appreciation.

I visited the University of California at Davis, the world centre for the scientific study of wine. They told me that their techniques, developed by the purest research and the most sensitive instruments, frequently produced the same results that the winemakers of, say, Burgundy and Bordeaux had worked out for themselves hundreds of years ago.

There should be a certain mystique attached to wine. This is not the same as mystery. But wine is not produced like fish fingers (or at least, good wine isn't) and slung into bottles; it is the result of an amazing cooperation between man and nature. It requires not only the right soil and the right weather but

a remarkable range of skills from the people who make it.

Obviously science plays a huge part in the operation these days; even wines that will go on to cost many pounds a bottle often start life in stainless-steel vats with an array of knobs and dials that would baffle an airline pilot. But there is as yet no substitute for years of experience and gut feel.

I visited the University of California at Davis, the world centre for the scientific study of wine. They told me that their techniques, developed by the purest research and the most sensitive instruments, frequently produced the same results that the winemakers of, say, Burgundy and Bordeaux had worked out for themselves hundreds of years ago. Making a fine wine, whether one that will retail at £5 or £3,800, is as much a matter of instinct as instruction.

Great artists don't do painting-by-numbers and great chefs don't follow recipe books; instead they know in their heads what will taste wonderful, what ingredient will work with another ingredient, where it should be cooked and for how long. In the same way, a winemaker has a sense of his land and his grapes, and he knows how to treat them both with all the right care and attention. (If you want to know what agony winemaking can be, read Patricia Atkinson's book, *The Ripening Sun*. She bought a property with vines in Bergerac, and what began as a hobby started horribly before she turned it into a successful and highly esteemed winery. The book is also very funny.)

People sometimes ask me what my favourite wine is, and the only possible answer is, 'I don't know – I haven't drunk it yet.'

People are afraid of wine. They often think they'll look silly in the eyes of people who know about it, and so they sometimes stick unnecessarily to the so-called rules. But most of the rules are there to be torn up. For example, lots of light red wines go very well with fish. And some red wines can be chilled. It's often a mistake to drink a pudding wine with pudding; they actually cancel out and spoil the sweetness of each other.

You don't have to drink dry white wine with Indian food; a rich and spicy red often goes better. Most of all you should trust your own taste. If a hundred people tried, say, Nottage Hill Cabernet against Parker's Terra Rossa – both Australian wines – 99 of them would probably prefer the second.

That's not because they have hypersensitive and highly educated palates; it's simply because the Terra Rossa has a better taste. It's not just a pleasant and perfectly good-value drink, like the Nottage Hill; it is rich and complex, and delicious in many different ways at the same time. Nearly all of us love fish and chips, but you don't have to be a gastronomic snob to prefer lobster Newburg when you can get it.

People sometimes ask me what my favourite wine is, and the only possible answer is, 'I don't know – I haven't drunk it yet.' Not being in a job that pays an annual bonus, and having no Russian billionaires among my acquaintances, I've tried only a handful of the really expensive bottles.

And, of course, enjoying wine is just as much about where you are and who you're with. A crummy bottle of French supermarket wine – and believe me, there are some horrors on the shelves of French supermarkets – can taste like nectar if you're in the flower-festooned shade of a garden in southern France, with cold meats, cheese and fresh baguettes in front of you, and good friends all around. The saddest scene in the wine film *Sideways*, when the hero drinks his precious Cheval Blanc '61 from a plastic cup in a diner to wash down fried onion rings, is the classic example of not matching the bottle to the occasion.

Many of us have enjoyed retsina in a taverna on a Greek island with moussaka or *dolmades*. But we'd no more take it home to serve guests in winter than we'd offer them Tizer with their beef Wellington.

So I've been lucky. I have had some great wine experiences: enjoying superb Burgundies in the Clos de Vougeot and the Hospice de Beaune; I've drunk Latour straight from the barrel at the château, and Château Palmer with lunch at Château Palmer. I've drunk 1900 Cockburn's Port, and sipped 1929 Volnay. I've joined Robert Mondavi as he worked his way through the 300 different wines from round the world that he tasted every single day, and I've slurped vintage Pol Roger in the sun-filled courtyard of the Pol Roger mansion.

These were great events in anyone's wine-loving life, but they are no more stunning than a magnum of luscious Saint-Chinian (costing a fraction of the price of any of those above) at Christmas Eve dinner with the family, or a Puligny-Montrachet on somebody's special birthday, or a Ribera del Duero served with minute steaks and salsa straight from a friend's outdoor grill. Or cold Jackson Sauvignon Blanc at a country picnic on a bee-loud summer afternoon. I could go on – almost any of us could go on, swapping memories of times when the wine seemed to set a seal on our perhaps temporary bliss. And good wine is available to almost everyone.

There are many great wines, and you'll find a few on these pages. These are wines you might select for the parental table at your daughter's wedding, or your own 25th wedding anniversary. But there are also thousands and thousands of others that cost much less, yet can make a fine occasional, memorable, and a special moment in your life wonderful. I hope they bring you as much pleasure – and sometimes joy – as they have so often brought to me.

Simon Hoggart
London 2012

Simon's Top Ten Wines

An agonizing choice, but here, after long and painful thought, are my top ten wines – arranged alphabetically rather than in order of merit, and with absolutely no disrespect to all the others!

Bâtard-Montrachet Grand Cru, white Burgundy, France (page 22, www.louislatour.com)

Château Climens, sweet white wine from Barsac, France (page 40, www.chateau-climens.fr)

Condrieu, superb Viognier, France (page 43, www.domaine-georges-vernay.fr)

Côte-Rôtie, the finest red Rhônes, France (page 50, www.guigal.com)

Ornellaia, magnificent red from Tuscany (page 105, www.ornellaia.com)

Château Pichon-Longueville Baron, first-rate Bordeaux, France (page 120, www.pichonbaron.com)

Pol Roger, one of the grandest of the *grandes marques*, France (page 124, www.polroger.co.uk)

Ridge California Monte Bello, the wine that won the Judgement of Paris (see page 84): superlative California Cabernet Sauvignon and blend, USA (page 132, www.ridgewine.com)

Parker Coonawarra Estate Terra Rossa Cabernet Sauvignon, incredible red wine from Australia (page 152, www.parkercoonawarraestate.com)

Domaine Zind-Humbrecht Gewurztraminer, glorious Alsace wine, France (page 170, www.zindhumbrecht.fr, but see 'How to Find the Wines Mentioned in This Book' on page 172)

Lovely, with the
fruit and the acid
in balance

TIM ADAMS RIESLING
Clare Valley, South Australia
WHITE ✪—✪✪

Tim Adams is a good example of an Aussie winemaker who started from almost nowhere, first working as a lowly assistant or 'cellar rat', spending five years doing a mail-order course in winemaking, then going on to university to get a degree in the topic and finally buying his own vineyard in the Clare Valley, South Australia.

The first harvest, in 1988, produced ten tonnes of grapes. Now he harvests more than 500 tonnes of Grenache, Sémillon, Syrah, Cabernet and Riesling, which is the one I tried and loved when Tim was on a visit to the UK. We had it with a whole roast suckling pig at the celebrated St John restaurant in London. (Slogan: 'nose to tail eating', and they mean it. The menu entirely eschews flowery descriptions and offers 'tongue', 'whelks' or 'tomatoes'. I don't recall being offered 'spleen' or 'gall bladder', though no doubt chef Fergus Henderson will get round to them.)

The Riesling is lovely, with the fruit and the acid in balance, so that it cuts through the fattiness of the pork without dulling the delicate flavour of the meat. If you didn't think about the cute little baby piglet as you crunched your way through its crisp but paper-thin skin, you could have a really good time.

ALBARIÑO
Galicia, Spain
WHITE ✪—✪✪

Crisp, light and utterly refreshing wine from the same grape variety as Vinho Verde

Decades ago, after the Lancaster House Agreement, I covered the difficult transition of Rhodesia to Zimbabwe. (Difficult, of course, but paradisiacal compared to what came later.) During the years of sanctions, the Rhodesians had discovered how to make the alcoholic drinks they weren't able to buy. There was whisky (distilled cane sugar flavoured with malt), gin (distilled cane sugar flavoured with something or other) and pastis (distilled cane sugar flavoured with aniseed). The last was particularly awful. Diluted with green cream soda, it made a drink known locally as 'kudu piss', which fluoresced alarmingly in the dark.

So it was wonderful to get real wine and, because the former Portuguese colony Angola was next door, we could occasionally secure a supply of Vinho Verde. This was crisp, light and utterly refreshing in the African heat. I wouldn't be in such haste to buy it now, since it seems somewhat acidic and is definitely short on alcohol. But I would most definitely go for the same grape variety made in Galicia, Spain, the region just above Portugal's northern border.

Albariño was virtually unknown outside Galicia even 20 years ago, when peasants grew small amounts purely for their own consumption. Now, helped along by the craze for 'anything but Chardonnay', it has become quite fashionable all around the world. It is rather like a more masculine version of Viognier, being pleasingly perfumed but with a stronger undercurrent. The good ones are utterly delicious, and most usually come from the Rías Baixas area.

As with so many wines, you get what you pay for; a pricey bottle is likely to be full, rich and perfumed. Cheaper ones can be a little thin and even acidic.

They used to be drunk very young, but recent technical advances mean some of them (the pricier ones, of course) can be left to mature and develop more flavours. Mind you, kudu piss had plenty of flavour. You just wouldn't want to have it in your mouth.

During the years of sanctions, the Rhodesians had discovered how to make the alcoholic drinks they weren't able to buy... The 'pastis' was particularly awful. Diluted with green cream soda, it made a drink known locally as 'kudu piss' which fluoresced alarmingly in the dark.

AMBRIEL BRUT CLASSIC CUVÉE NV
West Sussex, England
SPARKLING ✪✪✪

A fabulously, decadently sweet sparkler

JR

The recent dramatic rise of English wines that Simon talks about on pages 56 to 57 continues apace and the sparklers in particular gain plaudits, fans and awards wherever they are tasted. Make no mistake: they are now amongst the finest fizzes in the world, including champagne.

We have the know-how and we have a crop of talented young winemakers (thanks largely to the excellent winemaking courses at Plumpton College in Sussex); we have the investment and, in the south east of England especially, we have the climate (it's as warm here as it was in Champagne twenty-plus years ago) and we have the terroir. Why else would Champagne Taittinger recently have bought 69 hectares in Kent? We also have better label and bottle design and – crucially – the support of a new generation of top sommeliers keen to list fine English fizz.

Cast-iron favourites of mine fairly newly strutting their stuff include Herbert Hall Winery in Kent, Coates & Seely in Hampshire and Ambriel in West Sussex where Wendy Outhwaite QC, a leading barrister, now enjoys a hugely successful second career making first-rate fizz.

The Ambriel range is hard to beat, consisting of the Classic Cuvée, the Blanc de Noirs, the outrageously drinkable English Rosé and the English Reserve Demi-Sec, a fabulously, decadently sweet sparkler that is as fine a partner as I have yet come across for such English classics as smoked eel starters, goat's cheese tarts, strawberries and cream, Eton Mess, wedding cake or – and I'm only guessing here, of course – al fresco seductions.

CHÂTEAU ANGLUDET
Margaux, Bordeaux, France
RED ✪✪—✪✪✪

Good-value Margaux
with the flavour of
a fine claret

I have had a soft spot for Château Angludet for a long time now. I had gone to visit the property for an article I was writing about Bordeaux. There I met a gnarled winemaker who regretted the passing of the old times. As we stood outside the *chais*, or sheds, close to the lovely Girondin house that resides near to a burbling stream, he spoke bitterly about the kind of people they were now obliged to employ at harvest-time. 'Students!' he said. 'In the old days we could still get local people. For breakfast they had sausage, and a bottle of wine. This lot expect' – and here the greatest scorn came into his voice – '*croissants*, and *coffee*!' Had the young persons demanded vintage champagne and caviar sandwiches to kick-start their back-breaking day, he could not have been more outraged.

Most people agree that Angludet should be listed as a 'classed growth', and that some inferior wines are still up there after more than 150 years. But this is good news for us, because wine-buying is often dominated by notional prestige: the fact that Angludet can't call itself a 'fifth growth', or a 'third growth' or whatever, has kept its price down comfortably. Happy drinkers speak about spices, blackcurrants and blackberries, and praise the wine's great delicacy. You can also expect it to go on improving for around ten years or so.

Of course those old-time grape-pickers didn't get it to drink with their breakfast sausage; it would have been *vin ordinaire* from any old property. That way you only got your hangover *after* breakfast.

'In the old days we could still get
local people. For breakfast they
had sausage, and a bottle of wine.
This lot expect' – and here the
greatest scorn came into his voice
– '*croissants*, and *coffee*!'

ARNALDO-CAPRAI GRECANTE GRECHETTO DEI COLLI MARTANI
Umbria, Italy
WHITE ○○

Deliciously scented with peaches, nuts, and greengages

Umbria is the little brother, the Rutland if you like, to Tuscany, the original Chiantishire, where for decades now Britons have escaped to the bliss of Italian summers in the hills and the horrors of Italian bureaucracy. Not a great deal of good wine is made there, though in Etruscan times it was famous for its vineyards, as a good road network (for the times) enabled the growers to sell it outside the local area. During the Renaissance, wines from Montefalco, a hilltop town, were so highly esteemed that single bottles were sent out as tributes to the great and powerful.

Umbrian wine has also benefited from some serious technological advances. This is the kind of bottle that would make any expat think was worth all those months wrestling with planning permission and water licences. Arnaldo Caprai is something of a legend in the area, and he has produced a wonderfully deep, rich wine, minerally, but with terrific flavours of peaches, herbs, nuts and greengages. Also undergrowth, which sounds awful, but isn't.

Even if you drink this at home in winter, you can feel the warm evening sun on mellow stone, see the lizards scampering into the walls, watch the cypress trees and olive groves darken in the dusk, and think, 'Sod the crooked bastards in the council office. This makes it all worthwhile.'

A.A. BADENHORST FAMILY WHITE BLEND
Swaartland, South Africa
WHITE ○○○

An extraordinary wine that teases and tantalizes

One of the best things about New World wines is that they're subject to many fewer rules and regulations than those of the Old World.

Of course, the very term New World is a patronizing misnomer. Australia, for example, has several wineries dating back to the early nineteenth century (Penfolds, established in 1844, even boasts the oldest fruit-bearing Cabernet Sauvignon vines in the world), whilst South Africa's oldest winery – Groot Constantia – dates back to 1685. The point is, though, that winemakers in countries such as Chile, Argentina, Australia, New Zealand and South Africa can plant more or less what they want, where they want and how they want. And if they want to irrigate, say, by and large they can and ditto if they want to blend this with that.

So it is that Adi Badenhorst, who found fame as winemaker at Rustenberg in Stellenbosch (founded in 1682, incidentally), is able to make utterly bonkers blends with his cousin Hein at Badenhorst Family Wines. On paper, such blends don't work (and would be strictly *verboten* in Europe) but in practice they work like a dream.

My favourite Badenhorst wine and one of my favourite wines, period, is the simply-titled White Blend. I first came across it in the Saxon Hotel in Johannesburg. Knackered after a day's travelling, I was completely stumped as to what to drink and asked the sommelier for something cold, white, with plenty of character. She more than delivered and the first sip fair knocked my socks off. I've been a devoted fan ever since.

The exact blend changes each vintage although Chenin Blanc always remains at its heart. The current (2013) vintage is such a daft mix that I must tell you what's in it: Chenin Blanc (35%), Grenache Blanc (10%), Roussanne (9%), Viognier (9%), Verdelho (8%), Marsanne (8%), Grenache Gris (7%), Clairette Blanche (7%), Palomino (5%), Chardonnay (2%). Adi tells me that there's also some Semillon which he forgot about.

It's an extraordinary wine that teases and tantalizes like an elusive woodland sprite. Each sip is different depending how far down the bottle you are or how warm or cold your glass. It's intriguing, rewarding and utterly charming.

BÂTARD-MONTRACHET GRAND CRU

Burgundy, France

WHITE ✪✪✪✪✪

Incredibly powerful perfumed white wine

Here's a tip if you ever find yourself at a big commercial wine tasting, as you very well might one day. If they extend over the lunch period, there is usually food served to both visitors and exhibitors. It's rarely very good; more likely it's a buffet with, say, lasagne, or cold meat, or a few salads. Naturally most of the people ranged behind the stalls want to eat with each other, so they wander off leaving anyone to help themselves from unmanned stalls for half an hour or so.

This is when you (or at least I) strike. Some years ago, at a big tasting of Burgundies, I sampled a Bâtard-Montrachet. The marked price for the trade indicated that it would sell to the public for around £150-£180 a bottle. It was quite magnificent. It's very rare that you can say of a wine that it transports you. It doesn't just taste very, very nice, but it seems to travel directly to a different part of your brain to register a sensory experience unlike any that you have had before.

It was one of those unique moments in which the commonplace disappears, if only for a short time: sitting in King's College Chapel, listening to the opening notes of *Once in Royal David's City* (a cheat, this, since they tape the first verse, in case the boy singing has an attack of nerves, so maybe Kiri Te Kanawa hitting the first notes of *One Fine Day* instead). Or, when you first clap eyes on the Grand Canyon, infinitely more thrilling than any photograph can convey. Or see a quite breathtakingly beautiful girl walking down the street. These moments are rare, and to be cherished.

Which, of course, is why I waited for lunch to begin, and the table to empty. I could drink a whole glass of the wine, perhaps nearly £30 worth, in a few gulps! I guiltily poured and took the first few gorgeous sips. It had all the qualities of a great white Burgundy: peaches, vanilla, hazelnuts, flowers, cream. But it had an extra dimension, a strength and a purity and a richness which seemed not just to reach the palate but for a moment to affect one's whole body.

Bâtard-Montrachet is the little brother of Montrachet, greatest of all white Burgundies and, some would argue, greatest of all white wines, anywhere. Dr Lavalle, who in the 1850s ranked all the main growths of the region, said that whatever you were asked for a bottle of Montrachet, it was still a bargain. That may not be the case now, as the prices are Russian-oligarch high, but it gives you some idea of the intense adoration and loyalty the wine attracts. The Bâtard is hardly a wine to knock back with a fish-and-chip supper, but it is slightly more affordable than Montrachet, and would be perfect for a very special occasion indeed. Imagine it chilled but not iced, served with a very fresh lobster, shared for an anniversary.

These thoughts were going through my mind when the people came back to the table, and greeted me in friendly fashion, not knowing how happy they had made me for a blissful ten minutes.

BEAUJOLAIS
Burgundy, France
RED ✪–✪✪

Almost everyone remembers them: the little signs on
restaurant and wine bar tables, announcing *Le Beaujolais
Nouveau est arrivé!* They flowered in late November, and
for years there were jolly competitions to see who could get
their supply from the vineyards to London the quickest.
Merchants, restaurateurs and fans came by fast car, train –
or even private plane – to win the annual race and plonk on
our tables a fluid that had been grapes on the vine a couple
of months back.

Was it worth it? Possibly not. At one time Beaujolais
Nouveau accounted for half the Beaujolais crop. Some of it
was very good, and if you didn't mind playing the odds you
had the benefit of a very gluggable wine that is meant to be
drunk young. Beaujolais is made exclusively from Gamay, a
fruity, slightly earthy grape, with overtones of banana and,
in its youth, acid drops (the correct term is amyl, though
this brings to mind the drugs sold in some of our more
louche clubs). The acidity made it a perfect apéritif. The
taste buds kick into overdrive almost as soon as the glass is at
your lips. 'Bring us another bottle of this Beaujolais Nouveau,
landlord, and a Lyonnais sausage while you're at it!'

Sadly, a lot of Nouveau was pretty dreadful stuff. Some
of us thought it might do to clean the family silver. What
happened next is what happens to all winemakers who go for
quick profits over quality: they get swept aside as public
taste moves up a notch. People come to associate their
old favourites with the tacky, the second-rate and the
unfashionable. Beaujolais – *all* Beaujolais, including the
fine stuff made with love and dedication – went into decline.
Some merchants stopped selling it completely, or just kept
the odd bottle on hand for old-fashioned customers whose
tastes hadn't changed.

All of which is a pity. Some Beaujolais is gorgeous: rich, silky, combining all that fruit with a lightness of touch that makes it perfect for those tired of fuller, soupier wines. Ordinary Beaujolais still isn't highly regarded, even by the French. (There was a huge libel case a while ago, after a food and wine writer called it *merde*. He lost.) Beaujolais-Villages, made in 39 communes which sit on slightly different soil, is usually better. The finest are the crus, grown on higher ground. Many mature into lovely wines of considerable depth; the longest-lasting are Moulin-à-Vent, Chénas, Juliénas and Morgon, but I like Fleurie, which has that youthful zing. And for what other reason would you drink Beaujolais, even Beaujolais *ancien*?

BISHOPS HEAD WAIPARA PINOT NOIR

Canterbury, New Zealand

RED ✪—✪✪

Remarkably close to a fine French Burgundy

High up in the Waipara Valley in New Zealand there is a gigantic limestone pile known locally as the Bishop's Head. Does it look like a bishop? Of course not: no more than the constellation of Orion looks like a hunter. Still, that doesn't matter. It's near to the Bishops Head winery where Peter Saunders and Paul Hewitt make some quite splendid bottles. They learned their trade all over the world, including Europe, the USA and South Africa, and they tend to make their wines in a more European style than many other New World producers.

Their Pinot Noir is, I think, remarkably close to a fine French Burgundy. In their tasting notes they say that 'Our Pinot Noirs are punched down by hand…[with] a long, post-ferment soak to bring the tannins into balance'. This makes them sound like bar-room brawlers in a wild west hotel, soothing their injuries in a hot bath. I think I know what they mean, though: the result is certainly as distant from saloon-bar hooch as you could find anywhere.

I am also especially fond of their Riesling, which has that delightful floral flavour mingled with just the faintest whiff of petrol that all Riesling devotees look for. They reject with contumely any suggestion that their favourite grape brings the savour of a filling-station forecourt. It's actually delicious.

BORSAO CAMPO DE BORJA GARNACHA MITICA

Aragón, Spain

RED ✪—✪✪

This is a Spanish red made from Garnacha or Grenache, and I include it because I love the flavour, and because I like what people write about it. Take Oz Clarke on the topic of the new Spanish Grenache wines: '…a raw-boned power that sweeps you along in its intoxicating wake. It exudes a blithe bonhomie – all ruddy cheeks and flashing eyes.' If that doesn't get your juices flowing, try the English translation of a recommendation on the winery's website: 'Good step in the mouth. A wine with no faults. It is the first wine that I suggest to young people when they want to celebrate, with few means.'

The first wine that I suggest to young people when they want to celebrate, with few means

BRÉZÈME CÔTES DU RHÔNE BLANC

Rhône, France

WHITE ✪✪—✪✪✪

I love Brézème, even though it's a wine almost nobody has heard of. It isn't even mentioned in the magisterial *World Atlas of Wine*. All of it comes from a minuscule area just south of Valence. It is technically in the southern Rhône but shares many more characteristics with the north. As if that made any difference to us. The tiny region was almost wiped out during the phylloxera epidemic in the nineteenth century, but was rescued by a small number of growers who now make their wine with immense care from very small plots.

Rich, nutty, pears-and-apples flavour

   Most Brézème is red, made from Syrah, but I specially enjoy the white. The one I know best comes from Jean-Marie Lombard and it's made mainly from the lovely, plumptious Marsanne grape, with one-fifth Viognier to give it a nice, heady perfume. I offered it to an old friend, a former army officer, whom I would have expected to prefer claret, or gin, or whisky to something so delicate. But he was blown away by that rich, nutty, pears-and-apples flavour. It is not very cheap, but it is very good, and I always make sure we have some ready when he and his wife come to stay.

BYLINES SHIRAZ
McLaren Vale, South Australia
RED ❂❂❂

Flavours of liquorice, chocolate, blackberries, mint, spices and plums

I sometimes think, in a heretical kind of way, that the better a wine, the more difficult it is to identify the grape variety from which it is made. Merchants always have stories. One told me that he had invited a Belgian dealer for lunch. They always played 'guess the claret' with the cheese course – rather an annoying party game, in my view, since it can cause much embarrassment to perfectly nice people – and the Belgian identified the claret as Burgundy. When told of his mistake, he said angrily, 'That is because your claret *tastes* of Burgundy!' and stormed out of the room. Another sale lost, and well deserved.

Mind you, I once thought a Pommard, a terrific and pricey Burgundy, was a Bordeaux; I felt like an idiot. My confusion was only relieved by the memory of being at lunch at another merchant's where we were invited to try two decanters of red wine – each from the same grape variety but grown in a different area. A very famous wine writer guessed the grape was Pinot Noir. I did get that one right (it was Merlot), although I failed to spot the specific areas from which the wines came. But the famous wine writer wasn't to blame. At the very top end, each wine will have such a combination, so many subtle layers of flavours, that the characteristic taste of the grape is lost inside. Great wines drink alike.

Take this Bylines Shiraz. McLaren Vale is one of the great Australian wine areas, and the wine is pretty extraordinary. It is dark, dark ruby in colour, and it has flavours of liquorice, chocolate, blackberries, mint, spices and plums. Stephen Spurrier, the great British wine writer, says that the wines from this company (it makes an excellent Leylines Shiraz, which is medium-priced, and the seriously upmarket Songlines, which is £50 or more) may be the Château Latours of the area. Certainly the grapes, some from vines that are 100 years old, are superb, and many of them used to go into Penfolds Grange, the most celebrated of all Australian wines.

When you pour a glass you can catch the aroma from several feet away. The flavours are so dense and so intermingled that you wouldn't necessarily know it was a Shiraz. I suspect you'd have little doubt that it was an Australian wine, though.

CAHORS
Southwest France
RED ○○

Deep, dark, smoky and ripe

Before becoming a student, I travelled around France for a spell. The tedium induced by my own company and whichever book I was trying to read in French was sometimes relieved by the *bib gourmand* symbol in the Michelin guide: the tiny, red M Bibendum, the trademark fat man made of tyres, representing good meals for 10 francs or less. It was under £1 then, but even that was a special treat. I'd generally wash the food down with a tipple I thought I'd discovered: the black wine of Cahors, made in the valley of the Lot.

Since then I've been to the Lot many times, and have always been excited by its beauty, medieval hilltop villages, sensational views, and the warmth of its people. Like much local French cooking, however, the cuisine can disappoint. Restaurants need to learn that even tourists don't want *confit de canard* or *cassoulet* at every meal. And the wine known as Cahors? Well, that is a great sadness.

To my young taste buds, it was unlike anything I'd drunk before. Deep, dark, smoky and ripe, it spoke of summer days but also of damp caves and ancient cellars. It was elderly yet sprightly. I loved it. But not any more. The growers market it far too soon, when the raw tannins dominate and it's harsh. There's still a market for it; the French assume their local wine is the best in France – and hence the world. And the French drink their wine young, not like the British, who, in their view, leave it to moulder. But there is hope for us.

You can buy aged Cahors, although you're likely to pay 30 or even 40 euros a bottle. My friend Michael White, whose family owns a house on the Lot, started laying down good Cahors for ten years or more, and now it's delicious. The huge success of Malbec (*Auxerrois* in French), the grape used in Cahors, has energized some local winemakers.

One Cahors I like is Solis, made by Mathieu Cosse. It's fresh, readily drinkable, and if you can find it, it's well worth trying. Another is made by Sue and Mike Spring, an English couple who bought the Domaine du Garinet, a vineyard in the tiny village of Le Boulvé, just west of Cahors town.

Here they lead what looks like an idyllic life, enjoying the countryside, the food, and listening to Radio 4 by satellite. You can buy their wine at local markets, but it's probably simpler to drive to the vineyard (well-signed in the village) and, following their request, *klaxonner très fort* once you're there. They use new methods of vinification to make the wine drinkable earlier, although we bought some of their eight-year-old reserve, too, and that was scrumptious.

CASSIS

Provence, France

WHITE ○○

Nothing to do with blackcurrant syrup, this Cassis is a small commune on the southern French coast, very near Marseilles. It's a glorious and unusual setting for vineyards, and the local restaurants cater to the well-to-do: film stars, writers, politicians… many of them scoffing delectable rival versions of bouillabaisse, the celebrated fish soup-cum-stew of Marseilles.

The sea laps against the cliffs where the vines grow, giving a slight but perceptible salty tang to the wine. Only a small amount is made (roughly one-twentieth the production of, say, Entre-deux-Mers) and for that reason very little leaves the area. It can be found elsewhere, though, and while it is not cheap, it is very satisfying. The white wines, for which Cassis is most famous, are all blends, usually including Ugni Blanc, Clairette, Marsanne and even some Sauvignon Blanc. The most celebrated vineyard is the Clos Ste-Magdeline, with its stunning pink-washed art deco château. These wines are delicious now and, unusually for a white, will age gracefully for a few years.

Recently I found some bottles in a supermarket in Nice. After a glorious day in the sun, eating seafood in nearby Villefranche-sur-Mer, we returned to the city itself and drank cold Cassis with a few fillets of fish and some potato salad in our borrowed apartment, overlooking the Promenade des Anglais. It was bliss.

But you do not need to be on the Riviera; you can almost recreate the Baie des Anges at home. With a few prawns, a little smoked salmon and a bottle of Cassis, you can have the sensation of being a movie star.

CHABLIS
Chablis, France
WHITE ✪✪–✪✪✪✪

Austere and flinty background, with an occasional flash of green in the glass

Chablis is a wine that divides people. Many wine-drinkers adore it; they love that austere, flinty background, the occasional flash of green in the glass, and the hints of plump fruit that lie behind it. If they can afford £40–£50 for a great Chablis, a *grand cru*, they will get the vinous equivalent of a duchess: majestic, completely assured, superbly accoutred and likely to last forever. On the other hand, there is the phenomenon of Chablis rage. This occurs when you've gone to a downmarket restaurant and seen 'Chablis' on the wine list. The price of £16 doesn't seem too bad for such a famous name, and after all, it's someone's birthday, or your team just won. Then it arrives and tastes of nothing at all. Cold, thin and mouth-puckering, it resembles acidulated chalk dust. No wonder people feel they've been rooked and resolve never to let it happen again.

The answer is that Chablis is a name that covers a multitude of mediocrities as well as some of the greatest names in French wine. The *appellation* rules strike me as lax, which is why you sometimes see 'Chablis' on sale in cut-price supermarkets for less than £6. That can't be done without a huge loss in quality.

Chablis is grown on limestone soil southeast of Paris and north of Burgundy, and this gives the wine its mineral feel. On the edges, in the area called Petit Chablis, the soil is Kimmeridge, an English name, because the geological area stretches into Dorset. It is basically crushed oyster shells from millions of years ago, and may be the reason why Chablis goes so well with seafood. (Or perhaps not. You wouldn't expect red wines to be grown on prehistoric cows so they went well with steak.)

If you like Chablis – and it can be utterly delicious – then you just have to realize that you get what you pay for. An £9 Petit Chablis, from the outer rim of the area, can be sparky and fresh, and very agreeable drinking with a fish supper. After that, anything goes. Personally I've always liked the wines from Daniel Dampt, which usually bring a nice fruity undertone to go with all that steely limestone toughness.

Fragrant, flinty, smoky wine that is terrifically welcoming

CHASSELAS GRAND CRU CALAMIN
Switzerland
WHITE ○○

Switzerland is a very expensive country. Most prices are, I would say, roughly twice what they are in France, and the Swiss are happy to keep it that way. No riff-raff cross the border looking for a cheap weekend. It's also a country that has a very clear notion of socially acceptable behaviour. The apartment block in Zurich where men were obliged to sit down to urinate after 10pm (it reduced the noise) may be apocryphal, but any suburbanite can tell you the precise times you are allowed to mow your lawn. We once visited American friends who live in a village near Geneva. One of their neighbours stopped by to tell us, in a perfectly friendly way, that our car was badly parked. The back wheels were several inches further from the kerb than the front wheels. It wasn't blocking the street, which was wide, but it looked unsightly.

After Roger Federer, the Swiss person best known to the British must be the chef Anton Mosimann. I was once lucky enough to be taken to lunch in his club, where he recommended a Swiss wine of which his stocks were so low that it didn't even appear on his list. It was utterly delicious – and so it should have been, since it cost a fair bit. Only two per cent of Swiss wine is exported, and the Swiss are quite happy about that, too.

The finest wine (and the one Mosimann furnished) is made from the Chasselas grape variety, normally thought of as a pretty feeble fruit, more at home by a hospital bed than in a bottle.

But some growers, chiefly in the Vaud region, just north of Lake Geneva, have managed – through immense care and using very low yields – to produce a fragrant, flinty, smoky wine that is terrifically welcoming.

It's not grand. It doesn't try to make you realize how expensive it is, but you feel as if it wants to be drunk. The best examples are thought to be from two *grands crus*, Calamin and Dézaley, which you will enjoy hugely, if you can find them.

The back wheels were several inches further from the kerb than the front wheels. It wasn't blocking the street, which was wide, but it looked unsightly.

CHÂTEAU DE CHASSELOIR MUSCADET DE SÈVRE-ET-MAINE
Loire Valley, France
WHITE ✪—✪✪

Fragrant and refreshing, perfect with seafood

Muscadet used to be one of those words the dinner guest dreaded. We forget how common it was even 20 years ago for a wife to spend hours in the kitchen preparing a delectable meal with the finest ingredients. Then, when the guests arrived, her husband would take almost as long boasting about how little he had spent on the wine. 'Yes, it's from our little Greek grocer chap around the corner. He ships it in by the barrel, and you take your own bottles to be filled. Works out at around 67p a litre, and I think you'll agree it's not at all bad…'

Of course it was awful, as was most of the stuff other people brought in from the hypermarket just over the Channel. It is a pretty good rule that most cheap French supermarket wine is dreadful, and so is much of the pricier wine, too. At least the people who live in the north don't drink only their local *vin de pays*, because there isn't any to drink. But it doesn't stop them guzzling some pretty dire fluids.

The direst of the dire was Muscadet. Thin, watery, with an aftertaste of battery acid. Its only advantage was that it was cheap, so you could afford to neck enough to make you forget you were drinking Muscadet.

Things have improved mightily over the past few years, as this Château de Chasseloir demonstrates. There's no such place as Muscadet; the word comes from the Muscat grape, once grown in this part of the Loire Valley, near the sea. The entire planting was wiped out by frost in 1709, and replaced by Melon, which, despite its name, is a grape, from Burgundy. More care goes into the making these days. Much of it is *sur lie*, 'on the lees', which means leaving the wine on the dead yeast, pulp, skin and leftover grape by-product of the fermentation (and usually quickly got rid of in lesser wines). The lees add greatly to the complexity of the flavour, making for a far more satisfying, if costlier, brew. This Muscadet is fragrant and refreshing, perfect with seafood, but nice enough to drink on its own.

CHÂTEAUNEUF-DU-PAPE
Southern Rhône, France
RED ●●—●●●

Has that extra evanescent perfumed quality

In the 14th century, the Papal Court moved to Avignon in southern France, and the 'new castle' where the Pope lived still stands. For a long time the wine made here was simply known as *vin d'Avignon*. It was the 19th century before the growers had the bright idea of marketing it under its present grandiose name, and at some point the bottle embossed with the crossed keys of the Pope was added to the mix. The wine began to look like something which added lustre and prestige to the tables of the well-to-do. It helped that it usually tasted delicious.

Then, in the 1920s, the growers came up with the first basic set of rules for making the wine. This was the forerunner of the *appellations contrôllées* which determine and restrict how a wine may be made in order to qualify for the AOC label (now in the process of changing to the European-wide *Appellation d'Origine Protegée*, or AOP, designation). In fact, Châteauneuf-du-Pape has one of the most wide-ranging and generous sets of rules, largely because so many grapes and so many different styles were already being made in the area. The main grape used is Grenache, though at least half-a-dozen others put in an appearance. The result is that some Châteauneuf can be thick and soupy, some can be too tannic for agreeable drinking, while others are close to perfection: rich and full of flavour, yet with a wonderful lively scent as well.

I visited Zimbabwe a second time, not long after sanctions had been lifted. At Miekles Hotel, in what was still called Salisbury, they were selling diners the wines that had been imported before sanctions were imposed, and which had been lying in their cellars for a long time. Outside there were the first faint signs that, under Robert Mugabe, things were about to go horribly wrong. Inside, I had a half-bottle of Châteauneuf-du-Pape priced at the equivalent of £2. For serious drinkers in Zimbabwe it may have been the last consolation before their world fell in. There are many good and some superlative examples. A favourite of mine is Domaine de Saint-Paul, which has that extra evanescent perfumed quality and which sells for a very reasonable price.

QUINTA DE CHOCAPALHA
Estremadura, Portugal
RED & WHITE ✪✪

Quinta de Chocapalha is a winery in Alenquer, north of Lisbon. Like many Portuguese wines, it is terrific value, packed with flavours, yet light and zippy in the glass. There's an extra dimension of perfume here, too: remarkable, since it really isn't expensive. The estate is now run by Alice and Paolo Tavares, but centuries ago it was owned by Diogo Duff, a Scottish aristocrat awarded the honour of the 'tower and sword' (Torre e Espada) by King John VI – the only thing known about him.

CLARET
Bordeaux, France
RED ✪—✪✪✪✪✪

Like many British people, I feel just a little ambivalent about Bordeaux wines. (The term 'claret' for red Bordeaux is rarely used outside this country.) The good ones provoke admiration rather than delight, the bad ones disappointment. They are serious wines, not wines to make you gleeful. There are few that would, in Raymond Chandler's phrase, make a bishop kick a hole in a stained-glass window.

But there is certainly a long tradition of enjoying them here. Aquitaine used to be ruled by the kings of England, the wine was easily shipped to Britain from the west coast of France, and the taste for it has never quite left us. For some people it is the only taste they will recognize. My late father-in-law was a wine lover, and when he came to visit I would try to persuade him about the merits of Australian, or Chilean, Spanish or Italian red wines. Even wines from southern France. He would take a polite sip, then say, 'That's very nice, and I can see why you like it. Now, you wouldn't have any claret, would you?'

My doubts have several causes. Much red Bordeaux is, frankly, overpriced. Recently the Bordelais (as the locals are called) have become a little more realistic. Back in 1999, *Which?* magazine held a blind tasting of 39 clarets from British chains and supermarkets, and sweepingly dismissed 36 of them as 'very poor'. They reported that their panel thought them lacking in richness and ripe fruit: classic traits of wines that have been made to cash in rather than to please the drinker. The report was dismissed disdainfully in Bordeaux (they do disdainful dismissal very well there), but it certainly reflected the hidebound laziness of many growers, especially the smaller ones.

There was one year when enraged wine-lovers found that the Bordeaux they had bought *en primeur* (this means paying for your allocation at the time it is put on to the market, before tax, duty and carriage have been paid) were turning up in off-licences a couple of years later for less than they had paid. The makers of too many mediocre wines casually assumed that the huge prices commanded by the finest names would pull them all upwards. But the top names can charge top prices simply because they are top names. People might pay £250 to have a bottle of Château Latour grace their table, but that doesn't mean they will willingly cough up £10 for a bottle of thin, weedy, tannic, flavour-free Château Dégoûtant. And there is worse. Go into many a French supermarket and buy a wine marked *Vin de Bordeaux* for the equivalent of, say, £4 and the chances are that it will be almost undrinkable. If it has a sort of fruit flavour somewhere, that's a bonus.

And some of the famous names are not quite what they are cracked up to be, either. Often I have gone to tastings where grand wines in the top five of the classification system that dominates the Bordeaux trade offer a selection of vintages. You try something, even a quite mature wine from a good year, learn that it retails for, say, £80, and find yourself asking 'Why?' That money would buy you half-a-dozen bottles of a first-rate wine from several other countries – and the dirty little secret is that the cheaper wine would probably taste nicer. It wouldn't have the prestige, but it would have the flavour.

I know an elderly chap who has worked successfully in the wine trade for nearly all his life. I mentioned to him that, unless you had £3,000 or so to spare, it was hard to try Château Pétrus, famous as the highest-priced – or one of the highest-priced; there is now competition – Bordeaux wines in current production. And no merchant says, 'I know, let's pop the cork on a bottle of Pétrus, just to sharpen us up before lunch.' The chap said gravely to me, 'I have tried Pétrus on many occasions, and have never failed to be disappointed.' So, he'd be better off spending the money on a Persian rug, or a second-hand car for his daughter.

And if the British are picky, the French can be even worse. There is intense rivalry between Bordeaux and Burgundy. They are very different areas – Burgundy tends to be strongly Catholic, whereas the considerable British interest in Bordeaux (many trainees in our wine trade do a *stage*, or work experience, in Bordeaux) means that it has a more Protestant ethic. Burgundy is divided into tiny parcels of wine, often with a single acre owned by one person, so the wine has to be bought in and blended by négociants, rather than created in a single château, as it is in Bordeaux. (Incidentally, the term château is used very flexibly: it can refer to a fine stately home, as in Château Margaux or Château Palmer, or it can be a shed in a field. Think of it as meaning little more than 'property'.)

And the grapes they use are entirely different. Even if the wine laws allowed, a Bordelais would no more put Pinot Noir in his wine than let it down with Irn Bru. It isn't just the traditional, fun rivalry of Oxford v. Cambridge, or Liverpool v. Everton; it is deeply felt. Famously one celebrated Bordelais, Jean Lacouture, took part in a blind tasting on French TV. He said he liked a particular glass. On being told it was a Burgundy, he said, 'Burgundy?

Really? I had no idea. It's excellent. But just the same, I prefer wine.'

A few years ago, I had lunch in Épernay, one of the main towns in Champagne. Often, champagne growers serve you champagne with each course, in a doomed attempt to persuade you that it goes with everything. In fact, you wind up feeling bloated. These people served a Volnay 1926 with the lamb cutlets. This caused much excitement, because Champagne is a neighbour of Burgundy and a traditional rival – nearly always, if they serve you red, it's claret. So to serve us this ancient Burgundy was a rare example of reconciliation in action. (It tasted fine, though I wouldn't recommend leaving many wines that long.)

Writing for *The Spectator*, I do my best to find half-decent clarets at half-decent prices. It isn't always easy, but when I do I know the offer will sell well. There are a lot of people, even in this country, for whom wine means claret, and nothing else quite matches up.

How can you tell a good claret, apart from deciding that it tastes good? Well, there should be some undertones of cedar, and tobacco, and even leather. I think of it as being like the panelled reading room of a London gentleman's club, without the snoring. But even if it is old, it shouldn't *taste* old; there should be a freshness about it, a certain zing, a headiness, a nose that says 'Drink me!' like Alice's bottle.

You try something, even a quite mature wine
from a good year, learn that it retails for, say, £80,
and find yourself asking 'why?' That money
would buy you half-a-dozen bottles of a first-rate
wine from several other countries – and the dirty
little secret is that the cheaper wine would
probably taste nicer.

Stunning, almost indistinguishable from an Yquem at a fraction of the price

CHÂTEAU CLIMENS
Barsac, Bordeaux, France
SWEET WHITE ✪✪✪–✪✪✪✪

The great wines of Sauternes and Barsac are, perhaps, the nearest we will ever come to a potable version of liquid gold. They generally start in the bottle as a light straw colour, then darken to a lustrous yellow and finish their lives as a deep nutty amber. And the flavour! Rich and almost oleaginously sweet, they have an undertone of acidity that stops them ever becoming too sugary, and, as they swirl around your mouth and slide down your throat, you sense a heady, almost indescribable mixture of scents, savours and flavours. Here are a few, chosen more or less at random, that have been used to describe Château Climens: elderflower, honey, peaches, oranges, beeswax, quince, roasted pineapple, mint, toffee, chalk (how did *that* get in?), pepper, cream, morning dew and spring water, marmalade, vanilla, and smoke. You'd think there wasn't room in the bottle.

Some people say that the one thing you shouldn't eat with a pudding wine is pudding – or any dessert. The sweetness of the one cancels out the sweetness of the other. Better to drink them with blue cheese, or fresh fruit, or creamy pâtés, such as pâté de foie gras. If you must have them with a dessert, make sure it's one that is reasonably light – something with fruit, perhaps, or a crème brûlée.

I have chosen Climens because it often comes close in quality to Château d'Yquem, the most famous – and most expensive – sweet wine in the world. Experts can be easily fooled, yet Climens, depending on the year, costs a fraction of the price. Leave Yquem for the oligarchs; if you want to drink a wine of piercing deliciousness and also make your mortgage payment, Climens is the one to go for.

CLOS D'YVIGNE CUVÉE NICHOLAS
Bergerac, France
WHITE ✪✪

In 1990, a British woman, Patricia Atkinson, bought with her husband a ramshackle farmhouse, Clos d'Yvigne, in the Bergerac region. Their plan was to lead the good life of rural France while, perhaps curiously, running a financial consultancy. The house came with a small vineyard of just four hectares, and they went into winemaking almost as an afterthought.

A remarkable achievement by a remarkable woman

Nearly everything went wrong, very quickly. Patricia had no French, and winemaking in France is as bureaucratic as the Indian railway system. Her husband was ill, and spent more and more time back in London. A stock market crash put paid to the financial work. Her marriage ended and she had no money. The vines became crucial to her survival. Then her first attempt at red wine turned to vinegar, and she had to sell off the lot to make industrial alcohol.

It would be hard to imagine a more depressing start. Yet, with determination, and a lot of help from local people who clearly had decided that they liked her, she learned French, she mastered the paperwork, and she learned how to make wine. Over the years she has become not just a competent *vigneronne* but one of the best and most-admired in the region, making a range of white, red and sweet wines – her Saussignac dessert wine is especially good – that have already made their way into the snootiest French reference books and into many of the better British merchants and supermarkets.

Her Cuvée Nicholas is delicious, with its fruit, zesty acidity and nine months of oak all combining harmoniously. It's made from Sauvignon Blanc and Sémillon – the classic white Bordeaux blend – with some Muscadelle to add a dash of perfume. Like all fine wines, it is a heady blend of many mingled flavours, and you don't need an amazingly sensitive palate to detect peaches, cream, lemon, butter, vanilla and toast. It is slightly like a fine white Burgundy, but at a much lower price. A remarkable achievement by a remarkable woman.

LES COLLINES DE LAURE
SYRAH

Warm, silky, glossy,
rich and ripe

JEAN-LUC COLOMBO
LES COLLINES DE LAURE SYRAH
Northern Rhône, France
RED ○○

Cornas is a small *appellation*, or designated wine area bound
about by all sorts of strict rules, in the northern Rhône. It was
settled by the Romans. Some 30 years ago it was also settled
by Jean-Luc Colombo, a scientist from Marseilles who set up
a pharmacy and oenology lab. After a while he bought a small
parcel of vineyards and started making wine, which in this
neck of the woods must be 100 per cent Syrah.

He makes several styles, from different land and differently
aged vines. Some of these go on improving for decades and
sell for vast prices. By contrast, Les Collines de Laure (named
after Colombo's daughter) is, in the horrible jargon of the
trade, an 'entry-level' wine – which means it's the cheapest.

It is also the easiest-drinking now. I went to a tasting
hosted by Jean-Luc, and his finer wines were, frankly, not
ready. No doubt they'll be luscious ten or 20 years down the
line, but it was the hills of Laure I enjoyed most that night.
It is made from younger vines, which later will be used
for more costly bottles. Right now it's warm, silky, glossy,
rich, ripe and rounded, with a nice touch of vanilla, and
absolutely delicious from the day you buy it.

CONDRIEU
Northern Rhône, France
WHITE ✪✪✪—✪✪✪✪

Fat, gorgeous, unctuous yet zestful

Think of a wine that is almost unbelievably luscious, perfumed, packed with scents of peach, lychee, pears and mayflowers. With a very slight but agreeably sour tang to go with its voluptuousness. Or as one writer put it, like a sweet apricot tart with a great dollop of crème fraîche ladled on top. It's easy to get carried away by Viognier, a grape now grown all over the world, but it came astonishingly close to dying out. It's as if someone had found the last surviving pair of mating dodos and bred them so successfully that dodos were now almost as common as seagulls, or persuaded people everywhere to take up the Cornish language. In 1965 there were just eight hectares of Viognier vines left in the world, most near the end of their useful lives, clinging to the steep, stony soil of the northern Rhône's Condrieu area. In one very bad year, total production was around 2,500 bottles. The variety was about to become a historical curiosity.

It is a difficult grape to grow. Condrieu's basic soil is granite, but with a sandy topsoil known as *arzelle*. When rain washes this down the steep slopes to retaining walls, the wine-grower has to shovel the *arzelle* straight back up; otherwise his wine will have little of the heady Viognier flavour.

Over the years Viognier spread around the globe and became the chic wine of choice for white-wine drinkers bored by Chardonnay and Sauvignon Blanc. Some of this is very good, though Viognier should be drunk young (it grows flabby with age) and needs a degree of acidity to stop it being dull and flat. But Condrieu produces many of the finest examples: fat, gorgeous, unctuous yet zestful.

Today prices range from around £25–£50 a bottle; of course you get what you pay for. Georges Vernay and Philippe Guigal are the best-known producers of the finest Condrieu, but frankly it's all scrummy, and if you can find it, buy it, if only for a dinner to remember. Just outside the appellation is Château Grillet, also a Viognier, whose subtlety and richness make it every bit as good as most wines labelled Condrieu. It will last a few years, too, so it's not a bad investment – if you don't mind the initial cost, which is, ahem, on the substantial side.

HOW TO BUY WINE

BUYING wine can be a bewildering job. The London International Wine Fair is held every year in Olympia. Most years there are over 25,000 different wines on show there, all available for tasting. How could anyone start making a choice from all those? It is estimated that in the UK alone if you look hard enough you can buy wines from 32 different countries.

You might imagine that going into a wine store and saying: 'I'd like a nice wine. What do you recommend?' would be as pointless as entering a branch of Waterstone's and saying 'I'd like a good book, please,' or asking someone in Waitrose, 'Can I buy some food?'

Luckily the number of wine shops – even supermarkets – where the staff know whereof they speak is increasing. There's probably not much benefit in going to the immeasurably posh Berry Bros. & Rudd in St James's, London, and saying, 'Just want one bottle, mate, to go with the vindaloo tonight,' though their just as immeasurably helpful and well-informed staff might well suggest a rich red, spicy Côtes du Rhône, or alternatively a bone-dry Muscadet. However, you could go into pretty well any branch of any established merchants, including chain stores, and say, for example,

that you had half-a-dozen friends round that night and were going to serve them smoked salmon followed by a boeuf bourgignon. You wanted two bottles of white and two of red, each under £8, and what did the assistant recommend? You'd be unlucky if you didn't get a useful reply.

Incidentally, it's estimated that 90 per cent of the wine bought in the UK is drunk within four hours. This ad hoc purchasing can be fun, but you can save yourself a lot of money and trouble by latching on to a wine you like and buying a case or so. Of course, some people have nowhere to store it. Or fear that if it were there at home, sitting in the kitchen and saying 'Drink me', it wouldn't last very long.

By the way, there are few things more annoying than taking a really nice wine to a dinner party and seeing the host or hostess tuck it away for future consumption.

I thoroughly recommend shops that do tastings, and very many do. The excellent Majestic Wine Warehouse chain offers tastings every weekend, often showing a large number of wines, usually tied to special offers – e.g. £4.99 a bottle, or £3.99 if you buy two or more. If you find a wine you like there, I would snap up plenty. If you like it, the chances are other people will, too. Some merchants charge for their tastings, which I think is a bit grudging, even when the money you pay is refunded against any order you place. On the other hand, if the wines are expensive, it's a way for

the merchant to protect him or herself. Some customers can treat a tasting as if it were a drinks party, with generous portions being offered and drunk. Over the months and years you are bound to build up a knowledge of what you like – and what you like that you can also afford.

When I first got seriously interested in wine I kept a book (yes, I did soak off the labels of particular favourites and stick them in an album – a most embarrassing recollection now). If you add to the name of the wine what you served it with, who enjoyed it, who plainly didn't (in case they come again), how much it cost and where you bought it, then you've got quite a handy checklist for when you next go shopping.

If people bring a wine round to you, and you like it, don't hesitate to ask where they bought it, even if they might suspect you want to check up on how much they paid. Nobody was ever insulted by being told someone shares their taste. Unless, of course, it clearly says 'Tesco' on the label, or if you suspect that it's a bottle that was brought as a gift to them and has been doing the rounds for some months.

Look for bargains. Sometimes these are wines that were over-ordered and didn't sell. That doesn't mean they weren't any good; just that people didn't recognize them, and they now have to be sold to clear shelf space.

By the way, there are few things more annoying than taking a really nice wine to a dinner party and seeing the host or hostess tuck it away for future consumption. Some people are shameless. I recall going round once to a couple who were, shall we say, not exactly liberal when it came to the booze. So we took two bottles as our offering, only to see them carefully placed in a cupboard. The four of us shared a single cheap bottle they provided themselves. Total average intake per person over the three hours: one small whisky and one-and-a-half glasses of poor wine. I've never said, 'Do you mind if we leave now? I'd like to get home and have a drink,' but I've come pretty close.

One useful trick is to say, 'I've brought this wine because a friend recommended it. I'd love to see what it's like. I'm sure you've got your own plans for what to drink this evening, but I wonder if we could just try it?' Nobody is going to refuse.

Start small. You cannot grasp the whole world of wine in a week. Nobody can comprehend it all anyway: it changes too fast and grows too much. If you have an independent merchant near you, or a good well-run branch of a chain – the sort that trains its staff and keeps them – make friends. Buy, say, three different bottles, then go back and say which you liked and which were disappointing. That way they'll learn your tastes and be prepared when you show up again.

A lot of wine merchants are also wine enthusiasts and love the chance to chat to a customer who is either knowledgeable or would like to become knowledgeable. Talk to your friends, and ask what they've enjoyed. Obviously tastes differ, but less than you might think. If they've found a really great wine for a really modest price, there's a very good chance you'll like it, too.

Look for bargains. Sometimes these are wines that were over-ordered and didn't sell. That doesn't mean they weren't any good, just that people didn't recognize them, and they now have to be sold to clear shelf space. The same applies to the sales at the mail-order merchants. Often, in an excess of enthusiasm, they buy large quantities of a wine that is delicious. They print up a list which says, 'Try this wine. It is delicious.' But if people don't know the name, or the region, or the grape variety, they might still be suspicious.

For instance, I tried a Tunisian wine from a very reputable merchant. It was terrific, and a very reasonable price. But nobody was buying it. One reason is that a lot of wine is bought for social occasions. People are shy of plonking on the table something from Tunisia, or Uruguay, or Slovenia, even though the wines themselves are often first-rate. They think it just looks cheap.

Another thing to watch out for – and here you would need help from a specialist merchant – is overproduction. This is especially common in France, where very strict wine laws forbid specific wineries or districts to sell more than a certain amount under their own names. It's a very sensible rule, since the temptation to establish a 'brand' then stretch the quality till it snaps is always present. But it does mean that if there is a wonderful year, with perfect weather and harvesting conditions, the makers aren't allowed

Top 5 tips for buying wine

1 Try to foster a relationship with your best local wine merchant. They should soon learn your tastes and offer you good advice and deals.

2 Look for bargains: these may be being pushed simply because few customers recognize the wine.

3 Don't be put off by unfamiliar names and winemaking areas. They can often hide superb wines.

4 Beware ads for 'astounding bargains'.

5 Don't automatically trust 'big name' wines.

to sell all they make under its proper title.

Once in The Spectator we offered for £3.95 a red wine sold under El Vino's brand name, 'Velvin'. I was astonished how good it was. You could detect what it really was from the coding on the label – it was overproduction of Burgundy. Sold as Vin de Bourgogne it would have cost at least twice as much. Similarly in 2000, the very grand Bordeaux Château Ducru-Beaucaillou produced more than it was allowed to sell. The over- production was marketed as generic Saint-Julien, the name of the commune in which the wine is made. It wasn't quite as good as the labelled Ducru-Beaucaillou – naturally the very best grapes went

into the named stuff – but then it cost only £14.95 a bottle instead of around £130.

FromVineyardsDirect made the most successful offer we've ever run in The Spectator. It included bottles from a château which makes a third-growth wine, a claret most people believe should be a first growth, and which sells most vintages at around £200 a bottle. They get a little fractious if you name the original wine, but at £19.95, one-tenth the price, who is going to complain? You can't possibly be expected to know this sort of thing, but it is passed around the trade and it's another good reason why you should make friends with your local merchant or a helpful assistant.

Some people buy wines from schemes, usually in France. Often they are from vineyards set up by British people who need capital for expansion or equipment. You give them your money and receive the interest payments in wine, typically two cases per year per £1,000 investment, which can translate as a fairly generous 10–12% return. With £15,000 you could have a bottle per day in perpetuity. It's great if you don't mind drinking the same wine rather a lot. I prefer the variety, though I know people who are very satisfied indeed with the arrangement.

Naturally, I would love it if you bought your wine from *The Spectator*, mainly because we do try to select wines that taste terrific and don't cost too much. Several other newspapers and magazines make similar offers, and some are very good. Though we think ours is the best because we go to half a dozen or so different merchants in the course of a year, so oblige them to compete with each other on quality and price. What I don't really advise are those offers you see in the papers saying 'Astounding bargain! A case of wine worth £90 for only £59.99! Our fabulous introductory offer…' They can do this because they buy up the production of whole estates, vast quantities of generally mediocre

wine, which they can then flog off at apparently very low prices. But since they nominate the 'list' prices themselves, the rubric '£90 worth of wine' is meaningless.

There's an elderly lady near us who sells her own homemade scones, door-to-door. If she said, 'Today I am offering £6 worth of scones for only £3.50!' it would prove nothing at all, other than that she reckons people will only be willing to pay £3.50.

Subjects were offered a wine which they were told cost $10 a bottle. They were then given the same wine, served from a different bottle, and told it cost $40. Almost all said they preferred the second.

In the same way, you're probably only getting £60's worth of wine for your £60. The wines might have celebrated names – Rioja, Bordeaux, Muscadet and so forth – but that doesn't make them good. In fact, some districts (Chablis and Châteauneuf-du-Pape are examples) have pretty lax rules and some pretty awful wine is sold under those names. The cheapo supermarkets often sell wines under the same names, which I suggest you avoid. They also sell more obscure wines, and those can be very good value, because you're buying what's in the bottle, not centuries of publicity and, often, bullshit.

If you like the instant convenience of supermarkets, the two best are Marks & Spencer and Waitrose, which seem to alternate as supermarket of the year in the awards dished out by the wine magazine *Decanter*. Their choice, from cheap to top end, is pretty near faultless.

Though intriguingly, research in America in 2008 discovered that people adjust their expectations of wine according to price. Subjects were offered a wine which they were told cost $10 a bottle. They were then given the same wine, served from a different bottle, and told it cost $40. Almost all said they preferred the second.

A wine connoisseur in Norfolk once created great confusion among wine writers when, at a sumptuous dinner in his country home, he offered his guests four decanters and asked them to say what they thought was in each. After much discussion of Bordeaux châteaux, vintages, and so on, he revealed that they were all identical, and came from a bag-in-box Chilean Cabernet Sauvignon.

There is a lot of Emperor's new clothes about the trade. I've sipped mature clarets priced at £200 a bottle, and thought, hmmm, for that money I could buy a whole case of Chilean wine in the same style from the same grape variety, and probably enjoy it a lot more.

If you like the wine, memorize the name, and buy it next time. Or it might be more fun to try something new. That is the great pleasure of wine-buying: the worst that can happen is a mild disappointment, and you can have that joyful moment of finding something you love.

In the end, that is what the whole process boils down to: having fun, and having the intense satisfaction of making a find. Wine is for sharing, and for talking about. It makes you happy – partly because of the alcohol content, of course, though you could get that with cheap vodka – but also because it is the most delicious, the most complicated, the most beguiling and fascinating drink mankind has ever come up with.

Top 10 Wine

CÔTE-RÔTIE
Northern Rhône, France
RED ✪✪✪–✪✪✪✪

One of those wines which you don't just enjoy, but which imprints itself on your brain

This really is one of my favourite wines in all the world. It is not cheap, but that's because there isn't much of it. The French produce more than 300 times as much bog-standard Côtes du Rhône as they do Côte-Rôtie. But Côte-Rôtie has a power, a finesse and an elegance which lesser wines cannot match. It is a Jaguar compared to a Ford Mondeo. The latter is serviceable and perfectly good for its purpose. The other has a style, a sophistication and an almost imperious quality which it bestows on whoever is enjoying it.

Sorry, got a bit carried away there. Côte-Rôtie means, literally, 'roasted slope', as the vines are grown on steep banks on a bend of the northern Rhône, where they get masses of hot summer sun but are shielded from winter winds. The site is thought to be the place where the Romans first planted vines in what was then Gaul, possibly 24 centuries ago.

The two main parts of the hillside are known as the Côte Brune and the Côte Blonde. According to legend, they were named after the two daughters of the Lord of Ampuis, one of whom was dark and the other fair. It's nonsense; the names actually refer to the colour of the soil.

Personally I slightly prefer the wines from the Côte Blonde, because while all Côte-Rôtie is dominated by the Syrah grape, the blondies add just a measure – maybe five per cent, permissible up to 20 per cent – of Viognier, the greatest of all Rhône white grape varieties. This gives a heady, perfumed whiff to the rich, dark, earthy flavour of the Syrah and makes it one of those wines which you don't just enjoy, but which imprints itself on your brain, if you're lucky. And you can keep the best for up to 15 years.

COUSIÑO MACUL MERLOT & DOÑA ISIDORA RIESLING
Maipo Valley, Chile
RED & WHITE ✪✪

Cousiño Macul is in Chile's Maipo Valley, on the outskirts of Santiago. We may imagine that, until recently, all wines came from Europe, but that's not so. People have been making good wines all over the world for a long time. Here they've made wine since 1856, and they make a lot of wine with care and affection. I like their Merlot and Doña Isidora Riesling. I also like the label, with its wrought-iron gates. Labels matter, and in this case they mark a wine worth tracking down.

DESCENDIENTES DE J. PALACIOS PÉTALOS BIERZO

Castilla y León, Spain

RED ✪✪✪

Light and soft, but with a deceptive richness and depth

Few foreign tourists find their way to the small town of Villafranca del Bierzo in northwestern Spain as it is some way from anywhere the cheap airlines fly. It is a handsome town nevertheless, boasting some fine monumental architecture and a ducal palace. It is set in some of the most startling and precipitate scenery in the country – great hills and escarpments, banded by vines set on terraces and vertiginous slopes. The soil is pretty awful, consisting largely of schist, the kind of slatey, mineral-rich rubble that vines like. It was here in the 1990s that Álvaro Palacios, helped by his French-trained nephew Ricardo (the two *descendientes* of Álvaro's father), came to revitalize and recreate the Mencía grape variety, which had originally been brought to Spain by French pilgrims – Bierzo is on the path to Santiago de Compostela – and had been largely forgotten.

The Palacios, nephew and uncle, could see that the area was perfect for growing Mencía and set about producing a new wine from it alone: light and soft, but with a deceptive richness and depth. There is not much of it about. The price has been climbing, at first steadily, and now fast. It is the kind of bottle which, found on a wine list, alerts you that a serious wine lover has made the selection.

DOMAINE DROUHIN OREGON PINOT NOIR
Oregon, USA
RED ✪✪✪

Velvety, but full of life and flavour

Oregon is one of the loveliest of American states. Residents like to say you can swim in the Pacific in the morning and ski in the afternoon (though you'd need some pretty nifty driving in between). The mighty Cascade Range runs north-south through the state, with Mt St Helens – the volcano that erupted in 1980 and sent a cubic mile of rock into the atmosphere – just north of Portland, across the Columbia River. Twenty or so miles southwest of Portland is the state's chief wine-growing area, the Willamette Valley. Being quite a way north of California, this has cooler, cloudier summers than, say, the Napa Valley. But it also has milder, maritime winters. It is perfect for Pinot Noir, and the region has attracted lots of smaller growers, individuals with their own ideas and commitment, rather than the big companies that infest California. Their Pinots now rival fine red Burgundies, being slightly softer, earlier to mature, perhaps a little fruitier. They also command high prices, since Americans are proud of their wines, and willingly cough up for the best. The film *Sideways* also helped prices, since the main character's belief that Pinot Noir is the only truly worthwhile grape had a powerful effect on people who weren't quite sure of their own tastes.

Burgundy snobs might argue that the wines lack the austerity, the finesse needed for greatness. Phooey, say Oregonians, but with more conviction since Véronique Drouhin, from Burgundy's great Drouhin family arrived here to make Pinot Noir. The Drouhins bought their land (for what seemed a ludicrously low price compared to anything on sale in Burgundy) in 1987. Véronique was sent out to make the stuff. In 1988 she created the first vintage, with grapes bought in from outside, then in 1991, she made the first wine almost entirely from their own vines.

Véronique is as sparkling as a glass of champagne, and much-loved throughout the trade, not least because her perfect English goes with her warmth and charm. Domaine Drouhin Oregon (known as DDO) is velvety, but full of life and flavour, and every bit as good as many *echt* Burgundies. It's very easy to quaff – though you'll be lucky to get it, since Véronique makes only 15,000 cases a year. It is named after Véronique's daughter, Laurène, and if you find some I suggest you buy it.

The film *Sideways* also helped prices, since the main character's belief that Pinot Noir is the only truly worthwhile grape had a powerful effect on people who weren't quite sure of their own tastes.

JOHN DUVAL ENTITY SHIRAZ

Barossa Valley, South Australia

RED ✪✪✪

The best-known wine in Australia is from the vast Penfolds group. Grange is thought to be the finest wine in Oz. It is collected round the world and lasts for 30+ years, improving all the time. One of its makers was John Duval, who worked closely with Max Schubert, Grange's inventor. He also made some of the less expensive but still superb Penfolds wines, such as Bin 707.

Now Duval makes his own wine, Entity, slightly less powerful, less overwhelming than Grange with lighter, zingier flavours of violets and raspberries. He claims to lay his hands on the best fruit in Barossa, and he does create a velvety, harmonious wine. Here's the good bit: it's still ridiculously underpriced, simply because it is yet to have a world-famous name. It will. Right now you can grab it for around £20 – *if* you can find it; aficionados have started to snap it up. Wine investment is a risky business, and a lot of people come unstuck. But you'd do well buying this.

A lovely, velvety, harmonious wine

Terrific-value British
'Champagne'

ENGLISH SPARKLING WINE
England, UK
WHITE ✪✪✪—✪✪✪✪

A sleepy summer day in Cornwall. We're sitting on a handsome terrace overlooking the valley of the River Camel. Long rows of vines stretch down to the stream. It's an idyllic setting, quite the match of any vineyard in France, Germany or California.

And so is the wine. This is where Bob Lindo founded one of Europe's great wineries, largely devoted to some of the finest sparklers you will drink anywhere. You might imagine that a bottle of classy bubbles from Cornwall was as improbable as a meat-and-potato pasty on the menu at Maxim's. You'd be wrong.

Unusually for a *vigneron*, Bob used to be in the RAF and remembers flying in a Vulcan bomber over Buckingham Palace for the Queen's birthday in 1979. After he left the service he started to make wine, his first equipment including an adapted cheap fridge he had bought from Argos. After years of hard work and a steep learning curve, he managed to create a string of fine wines that won recognition around the world.

I first noticed Bob's wines in 2008, when a competition for sparklers was held in Italy. There are many of these contests around the world, and they're one reason why so many bottles have a sort of medal on the label: gold, silver or bronze. Most wine experts are sceptical of these occasions, and suspect that if you entered a drink tasting of sump oil it would sooner or later win a competition somewhere.

Still, Camel Valley's Pinot Noir had come second in this blind tasting, ahead of several champagnes and behind only Bollinger. That is pretty amazing. It's not easy tracking down a bottle, but I managed (by the cunning ruse of ringing the winery and asking for one) and it was well worth the effort. The wine is rich, toasty and complex, with flavours of fruit and nuts. It also has, in the words of wine writer Tim Atkin, 'a finish as long as an airport runway'.

A couple of years later I went to Camel Valley and met Bob. The winemaker these days is his son, Sam, who has several times won the UK Winemaker of the Year award. That is a gong seriously worth having. We sat on the terrace trying several of his wines, not all of them sparkling, and enjoying every one. I asked whether he would be able to sell some wines to *Spectator* readers, and he said he was sorry, all his production was already spoken for. In fact, he only had enough for the toast at his daughter's upcoming wedding; for the rest of the time guests would have to drink something inferior.

You can recreate our experience. Every week from early March to late October Camel Valley offers a tour of the vineyard, with a tasting to finish. There are two tours a week in August. If you are staying at one of the on-vineyard cottages, the tour is included, too. Check out the website: www.camelvalley.com.

Camel Valley is superb, and in 2012 it finally beat Bollinger in a blind tasting. Not surprisingly, its leading wine is as good as premium champagne at a fraction of the price. But, to be fair, the same is also true of Nyetimber, another English sparkler, which is made in West Sussex. The soil there is very similar indeed to that of Champagne, and the weather much the same, if a week or two later each year. They grow far less fruit per acre than is permitted in Champagne, which means that they can (almost) inspect every grape before it goes into the hopper.

I think Nyetimber's vintage wine is astoundingly good, bringing vanilla, brioche, peaches and even white chocolate to your palate. But it's also crisp, perfectly balanced and even creamy. It will cost you around £50 a bottle, so you might not be able to afford it for your daughter's wedding, either. But compared to its French equivalents, it's very good value indeed.

And while we're at it, there are several other fine English sparklers, such as Ridgeview and Breaky Bottom. They, too, are among the finest bubbles in the world, and we should be very proud of them. (See also Ambriel on page 17.)

ERRÁZURIZ WILD FERMENT CHARDONNAY

Casablanca Valley, Chile

WHITE ○○

It is languid on the tongue, the wine equivalent of a white-chocolate bonbon

I love this wine. It is the vinous equivalent of slow food, being left to develop in its own time. It is rich, and almost voluptuous. If you can imagine an alcoholic cream (well, you can actually – it's called Baileys) but one that has a real crispness and tang to it as well, you'll get some idea of how this tastes.

Like a child born into a privileged home, the wine starts with lots of advantages. The grapes are grown in the Casablanca Valley, Chile, only 20 miles from the Pacific Ocean. This means that sea breezes – and the Humboldt Current – cool the vineyards and slow the process of ripening by several weeks. That makes for more concentrated flavour inside the grapes by the time they're ready to pick. The rainfall comes almost entirely in winter, which means that the vineyards have to be irrigated with glacier melt as it pours down the rivers, and the process of ripening can then be much more carefully controlled.

'Wild ferment' is a technical term, but basically means that the Chadwicks – descendants of Maximiano Errázuriz, who are the present owners of the property – don't add commercial yeast to the grape juice, which is left to ferment itself. This makes for a slower process and thus the richer and more complex flavour. It is languid on the tongue, the wine equivalent of a white-chocolate bonbon.

LIVIO FELLUGA TERRE ALTE COLLI ORIENTALI DEL FRIULI
Friuli, Italy
WHITE ✪✪–✪✪✪

It is easy to imagine that there is little good white wine in Italy. That's because very little good white is sold in the average Italian restaurant, and when we want a really nice white wine to drink we're far more likely to go for a Burgundy, or at the cheaper end, a New Zealand Sauvignon Blanc or an Australian Chardonnay. The best Italian whites – and they are really very good indeed – need seeking out and are often costly.

One of those rare wines that lingers not only on the palate, but in the memory

Certainly Livio Felluga isn't giving his Terre Alte away with cornflake packet tops. You can easily pay £40 a bottle, and the only way I can suggest that you splurge on it is that if you paid £40 for any wine in a restaurant, it wouldn't be anything like as good.

This comes from Friuli, in the far northeastern corner of Italy. The area abuts Slovenia, which grows similar wines, on land often owned by the same people. The best wine is made by individuals, so there is much less danger of growers slinging any old grapes into the local co-op. Felluga's wine comes from the Colli Orientali del Friuli, one of the two best areas. He blends the local Tocai Friuliano grape with Pinot Bianco and Sauvignon Blanc, and produces a wine of intense strength and purity. It is floral, fruity and spicy. It is one of those rare wines that linger not only on the palate, but in the memory.

GAVI DI GAVI
Piedmont, Italy
WHITE ○○

It is still sprightly
and fresh and tangy,
and so great to drink
with Italian food

Some people are pretty snippy about this wine, which comes from an area no more than ten miles across in northwest Italy, just north of Genoa, and is made exclusively from the Cortese grape variety, which you don't see a lot of. The first 'Gavi' is the generic name for the district; the second 'Gavi' refers to the town, so that 'Gavi di Gavi' is Gavi that comes from Gavi itself. Except that it is now called 'Gavi del commune di Gavi' and it may or may not be better than just plain Gavi, which can come from any old place near Gavi. I hope I've cleared that up.

I love this wine because it has real body, and because it tastes of greengages, and because it is still sprightly and fresh and tangy, and so great to drink with Italian food. It is, it must be said, often slightly overpriced. This is because it is distinctively nicer than many feeble Italian whites. A good one also costs more because, to get the balance right, growers have to keep their yields low. 'Often a good wine, never a great wine,' say some of the experts, and they're right. On the other hand, if I see a bottle standing next to a big bowl of carbonara, or a rabbit linguine, or a pizza covered in cheese and cured ham, then I know I'm in for a very satisfying lunch.

GERMAN WINE
✪—✪✪✪

A century ago good German wine cost as much as the finest clarets. Now merchants find it hard to give the stuff away. I know when I'm writing in *The Spectator* that if I include a German wine in an offer, even saying, 'Look, this wine is superb, and it's amazing value', it will sell a few cases, but not many. You might imagine that some readers are buying it only out of politeness. Some people in the trade suspect that almost all German wine is bought these days by other people in the trade, who love it more than the punters do. El Vino, the famous Fleet Street wine bar (Pommery's in the Rumpole books) used to have a long German list. Now Germany accounts for just one in 5,000 bottles sold.

Why? It's hard to know but easy to guess. 'Hock' (after the region Hochheim) was once the drink of kings. People bought special hock glasses – rather ugly really, with a colourless bowl on a bulgy, ribbed green stem; you still see them in Germany and on the sideboards of older people here. Sales were affected by many things. At a time when bone-dry white wines are in demand, German wines tend to be on the sweet side. Even the driest (usually described as *Kabinett*) are sweeter than most dry wines from other countries. Then there are the labels, often written in Gothic blackletter, so it's hard for someone not raised in the German school system to read. And what can anyone make of something called Eitelsbacher Karthäuserhofberg? Few people are going to look at a bottle and say, 'Ah, yes, I see this is a *Qualitätswein bestimmter Anbaugebiete*. That should hit the spot!'

Germany also has 13 main wine regions, depending on how you count them, yet none mean anything at all to most wine-drinkers outside Germany. You know what a Rioja is, or a Burgundy. But whoever said, 'I've got a rather nice Rheinhessen tucked away for Jan's birthday'? Or, 'I know you love Nahe wines!' The Germans have now realized that this very complexity is harming sales, and have started simplifying their labels, sometimes with nothing more than the name of the estate and a brief description, such as 'dry Riesling'.

I personally suspect that another cause of plummeting sales was the marketing of huge quantities of thin, inferior, weedy, sugary, low-alcohol wines under various generic names such as Liebfraumilch. Some, like Blue Nun and Black Tower, were kind of all right, not bad, almost drinkable, but folk grew out of them and associated all German wines with predictable mediocrity. See what happened to Beaujolais after Beaujolais Nouveau fell out of fashion (page 24).

They tried an ad campaign a few years ago. Wine advertising is almost invariably awful. No, the French don't adore Le Piat d'Or – in fact 99.9 per cent have never heard of it. There was a tragic attempt to rid Bordeaux of its frowsty image with posters showing a gorgeous intertwined young couple dressed only in scarlet underwear. They might as well have written on it: 'Young people! Buy our wine and get laid!' The Germans produced ads showing 'Sixties hippies then and now' – 'now' being represented by a balding suited businessman. 'German wine has changed,' it said. 'Have you?' The implication that German wine was something you settled for in old age, like a deckchair instead of a beach blanket, can't have helped sales, either.

Yet there are some delectable German wines. (And let's not forget that in *Live and Let Die*, James Bond is offered 'as good a Liebfraumilch as could be found in America'. He replies, 'that sounds fine.' So we weren't so snobbish about it back in 1954 when Ian Fleming wrote that.) But you still need to know about the labeling. *Trocken* means dry, if that's what you're looking for. *Spätlese* means 'late harvest' – the wines are fuller and probably richer. *Auslese* wines are from even riper grapes, and need ageing. And so on, up to the rarities: *Beerenauslese* which is very sweet, and *Trockenbeerenauslese* which is incredibly sweet, incredibly delicious, remarkably rare, and predictably very expensive, so you're unlikely to see it in your local pub. If you want a German wine to offer with food, I would go for a *Kabinett*

QmP, but even then expect to have your guests complain that it's on the sweet side. It does make a lovely apéritif, however, and the fuller wines would go wonderfully with a fruit dessert.

Here are a couple of German wines that made me very happy. One is the Kabinett Erbacher Marcobrunn (See? It's impossible to pronounce already…) from Schloss Schönborn in the Rheingau region. This is made from Riesling grapes, and captures that perfect balance between acidity (without which the wine would be sweet and flabby) and sweetness (without which the wine would be acid and astringent). You could drink it straight away, or leave it for a year or so.

My own favourite is something of a curiosity. The Franken region is the home of the Sylvaner grape variety (written *Silvaner* there). This variety is not particularly well known or even well liked outside Germany. You'll almost never see it in the New World. But in the right hands it can make an amazingly delicate wine with fabulous floral flavours and crisp minerality. It's often compared to Chablis, though a Chablis as good as, say, Horst Sauer's Sylvaner would cost far more. It comes in the traditional *Bocksbeutel*, which looks as if the bottom half of an ordinary bottle had been steam-rolled almost flat. The wine you're looking for is Sauer's Eschendorfer Lump Silvaner Spätlese Trocken (Eschendorf is the name of the village, Lump the vineyard, Silvaner the grape variety – and the rest you know). It is utterly delicious, and my heart always leaps a little on the odd happy occasion I have a bottle to open.

GEWURZTRAMINER
Alsace, France
WHITE ✪✪—✪✪✪

It has an amazing flavour: voluptuous, spicy, full and heady

Years ago I spent a week reporting from the European parliament in Strasbourg. One evening a group of MEPs asked if I'd join them for dinner. In a car provided from their luxury fleet, they whisked us to one of the finest, most expensive restaurants in the city. The meal was exquisite – one superlative course after another – though I could scarcely enjoy it, since it was unlikely that the kind of expenses approved by *The Guardian* newspaper, my employer, would cover such an amount. Finally the monstrous bill arrived, and I must have looked queasy as I dug in my pocket for a credit card. This was greeted with incredulous astonishment, as if I'd stumbled into a Bateman cartoon titled 'The man who thought he had to buy his own dinner in Strasbourg'. 'My dear fellow,' said one of the MEPs. 'You're a guest of the European Socialist group!'

I can't recall the food, but I do remember that we drank a lot of the local wine, a Gewurztraminer. It was delicious, like almost all Alsace wines. (Strasbourg is the principal city in that gorgeous part of eastern France, which blends Gallic chic and German solidity. Almost everyone there has a German surname and a French Christian name.)

The grape actually came from Italy, around 1,000 years ago and its popularity spread north. Originally known simply as 'Traminer', it is still grown in many places under that name. The prefix *Gewürz* (with or without the Germanic ü) means 'spice'. It has an extraordinary flavour: voluptuous, spicy, full and heady. It has been compared, variously, to the smell of a tart's boudoir, and to Nivea cream, which sounds horrible, but isn't. It goes well with rich food, smooth pâtés, goose, some cheeses, with fresh fruit or just as an apéritif. Many people enjoy it with Chinese, Thai or any spicy Asian food. Those who love it (and I do) love it to pieces. You can't drink it all the time, however. It's a little like Oscar Wilde's wit: dazzling in modest doses, a touch overpowering in the end.

A few years later I returned to Alsace with my family. We had an introduction to the Hugel family of Riquewhir, which is a small town of almost impossible beauty, crammed with the fabulous painted wooden houses of the winemakers and merchants. Above it are the hills covered in vines; in the narrow alleyways you can taste and buy the local wine, as well, one might as well admit, plenty of tourist tat.

The Hugels are one of the leading families in Alsace winemaking and have made some of the finest Gewurztraminers for hundreds of years. We had a tasting in their offices, then moved to sit outside in a restaurant where we gluggled down more of the wine, while eating *tarte flambée*, which is a local dish: like an extra thin and crispy pizza. The sun beat down, the food was satisfying and the wine delectable. Some experiences are perfect in themselves and probably unrepeatable.

The other great Alsace dish is *choucroute*, which is basically spiced cabbage with meat. Loads of meat. There is an awful lot of *choucroute* about. The meat – great sausages, frankfurters, ham hocks, slabs of pork, chicken, anything the cook chooses to throw in – rests on a bed of this shredded cabbage with juniper berries stuck in it like tiny land mines. Six of us ordered a pot of *choucroute* from the mother of our landlady at the *gîte* where we were staying. It cost around £45, which seemed a lot, but it was so vast that, hot, cold or warmed, it provided some 49 meals before we finally threw the last half-pound of cabbage in the bin. All I can say is that it would have been a great deal more difficult to eat without the Gewurztraminer.

There isn't a lot of Gewurztraminer about. It is hard to grow, yields are small, and it doesn't fetch as much as it should, compared to the wines made from other classic but difficult grapes. Even the finest examples cost less than a white Burgundy of similar quality. Other countries, including the USA and Australia, also make Gewurzes, and some are good, but they tend to be restrained, perhaps trying a little too hard to stay dry, when the great ones let it all hang out in a terrific burst of flavour. Unlike most of the other great wine styles of France, Gewurz has never really been matched outside France.

The leading names also include Zind-Humbrecht (see page 170), Zinck and Josmeyer. The co-op at Pfaffenberg offers terrific value at a lower price. But there is some rubbish about. If you see a Gewurz offered at, say, five or six euros in a French supermarket, walk on by.

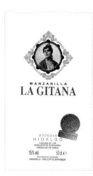

LA GITANA

LA GITANA MANZANILLA
Sanlucar de Barrameda, Spain
FORTIFIED ✪✪—✪✪✪

Simon is so right about sherry. Indeed, the comeback that he refers to on page 145 is now well under way. These days, sherry is even rather hip. Spanish cuisine is all the rage and Spanish restaurants and sherry bars are popping up all over the place. Even the top mixologists are incorporating sherry in their cocktails. And quite right too, for sherry has been woefully under-rated for far too long.

And Simon is bang on the money regarding Manzanilla. In fact I would go further and argue that apart from a fine demi-sec fizz or possibly – in a dire emergency – a dirty Martini or Bloody Mary, there is no finer 11am reviver than a top-quality Manzanilla, namely La Gitana from Bodegas Hidalgo.

If you can manage solids, pair it with bite-sized slivers of jamón ibérico that you pick up in your fingers as they do in Spain. Thanks to the acorns the pata negra pig eats as it roams free in the lush, wooded hillside pastures of southern Spain, this ham is sweet, rich and nutty, with a seductive creamy fat which melts on the tongue as soon as you pop it in the mouth.

And given that Manzanilla is packed with vitamin B6 (ideal for breaking down alcohol in the liver) and jamón ibérico is low in both salt (despite having been cured in it) and calories (only 190 in a plate of 100g of ham) but high in mono-unsaturated fat and oleic acid (which stimulate 'good cholesterol' and help reduce 'bad cholesterol'), this is about as healthy a mid-morning snack as you're likely to find.

Family-owned Bodegas Hidalgo was founded in 1792 and is now in the hands of Javier Hidalgo of the family's fifth generation. They make much else besides La Gitana Manzanilla, such as the richly nutty Amontillado 'Napoleon' and the full-flavoured but dry Palo Cortado 'Wellington', but it's La Gitana I keep returning to. It's light, delicate, bone-dry, slightly savoury, exuberantly fresh, wonderfully appetizing and ridiculously cheap. Little wonder that it's the best-selling Manzanilla of all.

There is no finer 11am reviver than a top-quality Manzanilla, namely La Gitana

JR

GRAHAM'S VINTAGE PORT
Douro Valley, Portugal
FORTIFIED ✪✪✪✪

Two hours' drive east from Porto, the River Douro flows lazily past the Quinta dos Malvedos, a fine white-porticoed building high on the bluff above the river. The house is surrounded by fruit trees – bearing figs, tangerines, oranges, lemons and pomegranates – and all around them, stretched out on steep storied slopes hundreds of feet high, are the vines used to make port.

The grapes, a bewildering variety of different types, are picked and placed in *lagars*, great shallow granite vats. Some port houses still get real people – usually local peasants already tired from a day's picking – to tread the grapes, as the human foot – being at the forefront of advanced technology – crushes the fruit without breaking the bitter pips. At Graham's, they have invented their own robotic feet, which stamp up and down in the stainless-steel basins. When the liquid is exactly eight per cent alcohol – the moment might come in the middle of the night – brandy is added to kill the yeasts and stop the fermentation. That is why port is very strong and very sweet.

Vintages are 'declared' only every three years or so, when the result has been extraordinarily rich and complex. Charles Symington, head of the leading family of shippers in Porto, says that the '94 is the finest vintage of the past 100 years. It is wonderful now, but will continue to improve until around 2018. Like all the great vintage ports it has a powerful, perfumed sweetness that seems to take over your palate, nose and even your brain. There are many fine ports, and connoisseurs have their favourites, but they all agree that this is a majestic wine.

It has a powerful, perfumed sweetness that seems to take over your palate, your nose and even your brain

ALAIN GRAILLOT
CROZES-HERMITAGE BLANC
Northern Rhône
WHITE ✪✪✪

The very best
Crozes-Hermitages
can be as good as
Hermitage

Alain Graillot has been making wine in the northern Rhône for some thirty years and he's quietly become one of the region's great names, making exquisite Hermitage, Cornas and St. Joseph, all silky smooth and bursting with character. He also makes a big-boned, robust Syrah called Tandem in cahoots with the Ouled Thaleb winery in Morocco (he met the owners whilst on a cycling holiday) and has recently branched out into Beaujolais at Domaine de Fa, making a wonderful wine full of succulent, ripe bramble fruit with a hint of spice.

But the wine of Alain's that I love most is his Crozes-Hermitage Blanc. It's a staple on the list of one of my favourite restaurants in London – Bellamy's in Bruton Place – and whenever I head there for lunch, however hard I try, I can't seem to wean myself off it. I almost manage to order something else but invariably fall at the last and plump feebly for the Crozes yet again, largely because I fear that next time I visit it won't be there.

Nearly all Crozes-Hermitage is red (usually made from 100 per cent Syrah but with a permissible addition of up to 15 per cent white Marsanne and Roussanne) and it's often thought of as a poor man's Hermitage (it's certainly a fraction the price). The Hermitage appellation enjoys the prime vineyard sites on sun-catching, well-draining slopes while that of Crozes-Hermitage makes do on flatter, rockier, more clay-rich soil. Canny folk know, though, that the very best Crozes-Hermitages can be as good as Hermitage.

As I say, most of it is red but some enlightened producers make a white and Alain's, from 80 per cent Marsanne and 20 per cent Roussanne, is a complete and utter joy. At the time of writing it retails for around twenty quid at Yapp Bros and is full of peach and apricot flavours, wild flowers, an elusive touch of honey and a deliciously savoury, mineral finish. It has character and style and is the perfect antidote for those bored – however temporarily – with better known regions and grape varieties. It's just that little bit different and, quite simply, has what we learned experts like to term drinkability.

TALKING ABOUT WINE

James Thurber's joke about the naïve domestic Burgundy without any breeding wouldn't work now. No one in America could have a 'domestic' Burgundy, since these days Burgundy has to come from Burgundy. Perhaps he would say, 'It's a slightly callow Pinot Noir, but I think you'll find it has a cheerful élan.' Or some such.

Wine writers are forever getting in trouble for the use of such over-the-top language. The wine expert who appears on television and chirps about 'peaches, lychees, blackberries, cedarwood, tobacco, and, mmm, I'm getting cinnamon' is a modern stock figure of fun, though you wonder what alternative there might be. Are they supposed simply to say, 'Yes, this is delicious. So is this. This is even scrummier'?

What you are looking for is 'balance' between the distinct tastes, and between acidity and sweetness.

Describing flavours in words is difficult, as difficult as using words to discuss music, and if you think some wine writing is pretentious, you should read the notes in classical concert programmes.

What makes a great wine taste great is the complexity of its flavours. The more the merrier is a general rule, though of course it helps if they blend together harmoniously. What you are looking for is 'balance' between the distinct tastes, and between acidity and sweetness. Nobody ever said to a wine waiter: 'My fiancée and I are celebrating our engagement. Please bring us your most balanced wine.' Though they would certainly know an unbalanced wine if they drank it – too sweet and cloying without sharpness, or too dry without any compensating richness.

A first-rate claret, for example, will have the expected cedar, leather and tobacco flavours in the background, almost as if you were sitting in an armchair in the library of a Pall Mall gentleman's club. But it will also have lively, fruit-filled flavours alongside. It's the combination of all these that makes a wine stand out from the pack.

Now, it is possible to become a little silly. One of the most ridiculous descriptions of a wine I ever read was for a Gewurztraminer. 'Top notes of vanilla, spice and lychees,' it said, 'with an undertone of Nivea cream.' Can you imagine ever telling your guests, 'You'll enjoy this; it tastes of Nivea cream'? Mightn't they reply, 'Oh, we were hoping for

But the slight, evanescent gust of
hot rubber can actually be very pleasant,
helping to set off and heighten
the other flavours in the wine.

something a bit more Oil of Olay to go with the lobster.'

Yet even there, the writer was making a point. A good Gewürz does taste slightly oily, in a pleasant way of course. That, along with the intense fruit and floral flavours, is what makes it a unique grape. The best Rieslings have a whiff of petrol about them, though they would only waft you back to memories of filling up the car if they were overpowering. The slight reminder of fuel, almost caught on the breeze as you sniff the glass, intensifies your glugging experience.

'Top notes of vanilla, spice and lychees,' it said, 'with an undertone of Nivea cream.'

Wine writers do have a lot of useful words to capture separate flavours. Most of them are very pleasing. Who wouldn't look forward to drinking a wine that included almonds, mulberries, morello cherries, chestnuts and apricots?

On the other hand, there are some flavours which would put anybody off. If your host handed you a glass of Shiraz saying, 'Get this down: it tastes of burning rubber', you'd probably ask for a cup of tea instead. But the slight, evanescent gust of hot rubber can actually be very pleasant, helping to set off and heighten the other flavours in the wine. Here are some other queasy descriptions of certain grapes.

'Pencil shavings' are associated with Cabernet Franc. It's a good description of one element in the overall flavour, yet the wine is still very agreeable. Old clarets are often described as featuring 'undergrowth'. Very sweet wines, which have acquired botrytis, or noble rot, have a hint of 'boiled cabbage'. Some people say they can detect 'bacon fat' in older Alsace wines, although the flavour that would make most of us gag is found in Sauvignon Blanc: 'cat's pee'.

Now and again, a wine writer will say that something tastes of 'grapes', but that is far too simplistic, and would be admitting defeat.

A lovely, luscious white wine

CHÂTEAU GRINOU
LA COMBE DE GRINOU
Bergerac, France
WHITE ⊙

I have a special affection for this wine. My day job is at the House of Commons, which at one time had a celebrated wine cellar. Then along came Robert Maxwell, who in 1964 became the Labour MP for Buckingham. The Refreshment Department, which is responsible for all the catering at the House, was in perpetual financial difficulty. One reason was that sittings of the House can be unpredictable, and were especially wayward in those days. A session that was supposed to end at around 11pm might continue till, say, five in the morning, with huge costs in overtime and taxis home for the staff who manned the many bars and eating places. Or the opposite would happen, and they'd have to pay the staff they'd booked while getting no revenue in. Maxwell promised to restore the department to profit. Which he did, by selling off its wines.

It was an extraordinary act of vandalism, for a great wine cellar is, in its way, like a fine library, even if the stock changes more often. It has its own history, and encompasses the history of all the bottles in it. Every time you order a vintage wine, you are reviving and enjoying a part of the past. Even though the wines Maxwell flogged off are gone, there is still a tradition of good drinking in the Commons, often at very moderate prices. Indeed, members and staff can reckon to drink for roughly retail price plus 50 per cent, around half the price charged even in the less-grasping London restaurants. A team of MPs helps make the choice every few years or so at a huge blind tasting. They are all wine enthusiasts but not necessarily wine experts, which in my view makes their judgement more reliable, since they are in touch with the public palate in a way that those who taste scores of wines each day for their living may not be.

One of their choices was this luscious La Combe de Grinou, made in Bergerac by Guy Cuisson. The white – my favourite – is half Sauvignon Blanc and half Sémillon, the richness of the latter complementing the dry, grassy flavours of the former. The wine was a *coup de coeur* (prizewinner) in the 1998 edition of the definitive *Hachette Wine Guide*, and they only give that to one in 35 of the bottles they try. It's a lovely wine, and if you can run to the Reserve, that's even nicer. Both are fantastic value.

A team of MPs helps make the choice every few years or so at a huge blind tasting. They are all wine enthusiasts but not necessarily wine experts, which in my view makes their judgement more reliable, since they are in touch with the public palate in a way that those who taste scores of wines each day for their living may not be.

HAMILTON RUSSELL CHARDONNAY

Hemel-en-Aarde Valley, South Africa

WHITE ✪✪✪—✪✪✪✪

Elegant yet restrained, confident yet unshowy, refined yet rewarding

Anthony Hamilton Russell owns more shoes than any straight man I know. Even more than his wife. He's nothing if not a dandy and is always immaculately turned out. There's an understated self-confidence about him and great generosity of spirit too. Indeed, Anthony and his wife Olive are two of the most hospitable folk I've ever had the pleasure to meet. And the Hamilton Russell wines are exactly the same: elegant yet restrained, confident yet unshowy, refined yet rewarding.

South Africa is producing some of the most exciting and downright tasty wines in the world at the moment and in the first vineyards to be planted in Walker Bay, in the Hemel-en-Aarde ('Heaven and Earth') Valley, just above Hermanus in the Western Cape, Anthony is producing some of the finest.

He makes a Pinot Noir and a Chardonnay under the Hamilton Russell label; a Sauvignon Blanc and a Pinotage under the Southern Right label; and a Pinotage blend and a white Bordeaux blend under the Ashbourne label.

It's the hand-picked, barrel-aged Hamilton Russell Chardonnay, though, that I come back to every time, lapping up its poached ripe pear, honey, citrus, butter, cream and toast flavours and its tight, mineral finish.

It's more than a little Burgundian in style and I remember a tasting in Beaune a few years back where Anthony put his wines up against those of Véronique Drouhin of Domaine Drouhin. Despite being less than half the price, the Hamilton Russell Chardonnay more than held its own against Véronique's fabulous Beaune Clos des Mouches.

South Africa has come a long way in the last several years. Try a bottle of this and see just how far.

HEGARTY LES CHAMANS ROUGE MINERVOIS

Languedoc-Roussillon, France

RED ✪✪—✪✪✪

Gorgeous, being robust, warm, and with that heady whiff of perfume

This luscious wine is made by Sir John Hegarty, of the advertising company Bartle Bogle Hegarty (BBH). He did ads for Levi's jeans, Audi, Reebok and other products you have probably heard of. He also talks in adman jargon. When the well-known wine writer Jancis Robinson went to see him he offered her aperçus such as 'black is only black when you put it next to white', or 'when the world zigs, zag'. You are unlikely to hear similar wisdom from the gnarled peasants working the land nearby.

Hegarty wanted to make a fine wine in the Languedoc, the world's largest wine region, and he selected the modestly sized Minervois *appellation* to buy his land. It was a very expensive undertaking, and he needed all he had of what he terms 'creative ignorance' – the insights that derive from coming fresh to a situation. Money seemed to vanish into the soil like autumn rains. The whole enterprise could have been just another rich man's folly, except that it worked.

He makes only 25 hectolitres of wine for every hectare of land – much less than is allowed, very roughly half the local average – and it is gorgeous, being robust, warm, and with that heady whiff of perfume that lifts a wine from being something nice to swig into something delightful to sip. Hegarty thrived in a trade that depends entirely on illusion, so it's nice that he has produced something whose quality can only be enjoyed, not cunningly implied.

CHARLES HEIDSIECK BRUT RÉSERVE NV

Champagne, France

SPARKLING ✪✪✪✪

An astoundingly
fine champagne

Pol Roger is quite rightly one of Simon's Top Ten Wines. It's one of mine too. Along with Bollinger. I love them both equally and to distraction and have drunk enough of both over the years to know that my adoration is no passing whim.

Occasionally, though, I find myself unexpectedly distracted from my Pol- and Bol-drinking by the come-hither looks and wiggling hips of another. And so it was recently with Charles Heidsieck Brut Réserve NV. I had not tasted it in ages, aware that it had had a bit of a dip in its fortunes and having also foolishly confused it with Heidsieck Monopole 'Blue Top', a lacklustre fizz that always seems to be on some dubious BOGOF deal in some supermarket somewhere.

Charles-Camille Heidsieck (1822–93) was the original 'Champagne Charlie', celebrated as one of the first to export champagne to 19th century America, in famously vast quantities, and for getting arrested and imprisoned as a Confederate spy during the American Civil War.

Quite by chance, a little while ago, I found myself with a glass of the wine that bears his name. And, blow me, it completely stopped me in my tracks. Indeed, I was utterly smitten. It turns out that it's an astoundingly fine champagne – as fine a non-vintage champagne as I've tasted in years – full of toast, brioche, caramel, butterscotch and white peaches. It has a far greater amount of reserve wines in its blend (some 40 per cent, with an average age of ten years) than any of the major houses other than Krug and it shows in its voluptuous, mouth-filling complexity.

Remarkably, despite its swanky new packaging and vastly improved blend, Charles Heidsieck Brut Réserve NV remains under most people's radar. It's one of Champagne's greatest secrets and whenever I now see it on a restaurant wine list I have a little frisson of recognition and realise that it's a secret that the sommelier is in on.

HENSCHKE HILL OF GRACE
Eden Valley, South Australia
RED ✪✪✪✪✪

Stephen Henschke is the best-known, and probably the finest, independent winemaker in Australia. His family has been around for some 160 years. They have an unusual background for the trade, having arrived as a result of a doctrinal dispute in Brandenberg, now part of Poland. King Friedrich III of Prussia wanted to unify two Protestant churches: the Lutherans and the Reformed Church, the latter much the smaller but of which he was a member. He also wished to be king and bishop of the new church. The Lutherans didn't like that; they thought it was overweening. In those days, when such matters assumed massive import, it was enough to send boatloads of Lutherans off to Australia, specifically to the regions near Adelaide. Henschke's most famous wine, a Shiraz called Hill of Grace, is grown on a knoll opposite a Lutheran church.

Over the years, Hill of Grace has managed to acquire that patina of prestige all winemakers would love to have: people will buy it to show off. For example, each bottle comes in its own wooden case, like a small coffin. I tried it at a tasting where it was priced at £150 a bottle. A wine expert more distinguished than me sniffed that it was 'more a £50 wine than £150'. But it is a magnificent wine by any standards. Deep and dark, it has to be sipped slowly to reveal the overlapping flavours. Some of the vines on the hill are 140 years old.

There is a tragic story attached to the wine. Hill of Grace was created by Cyril Henschke, one of the greatest winemakers Australia has known. In 1979, when he was 55, he was killed by his own wife, Doris. A celebrated murder trial followed. Doris, who that night had been glugging a copious variety of drinks, including ouzo as well as wine, and who was on several prescription tranquillizers, shot Cyril dead while he was lying in bed. She pleaded that it had been an accident; she had tripped while handing him the shotgun to deal with some noisy birds. The jury believed her.

Deep and dark, it has to be sipped slowly to reveal the overlapping flavours

Some South Australians hold that her acquittal ushered in a majestic era for the wines of their region. In any event, Cyril Henschke, a Bordeaux-type red wine named in his honour, is superb, and in some years can fetch almost as much as Hill of Grace.

Henschke also makes a wide range of other wines from other grape varieties, all very good, some extremely fine. I especially like Tilly's Vineyard, a blend of Sémillon and Sauvignon Blanc and 19 per cent Chardonnay, which is lively and zingy, and full of fruit, and costs an awful lot less than Hill of Grace.

Each bottle comes
in its own wooden case,
like a small coffin.

FRANZ HIRTZBERGER
GRÜNER VELTLINER SMARAGD
Wachau, Austria
WHITE ✪✪✪

Absolutely delectable

In 1985 there was a tremendous and damaging scandal when millions of gallons of Austrian wine were found to be adulterated with diethylene glycol, which is an ingredient of car anti-freeze and very dangerous indeed. Some growers relied on selling sweet wines to the German market, but a succession of bad summers had led to poor, inadequate harvests. The chemical added extra sweetness and body. It worked well, and many experts were fooled, though of course, in the long term it literally could have killed off the market. The scam was only discovered when an ultra-greedy producer tried to reclaim the VAT on the chemical.

A larger wine-producing country might have survived the affair more easily, but Austrian wines are not the world's most famous, and even now, almost a quarter of a century later, people casually associate them with the poisonous admixture. But the industry has made quite a comeback. Austria now produces some of the most subtle and delicious wines in Europe – wines that would be absolutely useless at helping your car to start on a cold day, though they might well buck you up.

Wachau is the finest wine region, even though it has only three per cent of the country's vineyards. It is in the east of the country, 40 miles or so from Vienna. The banks of the Danube are very steep here, so the area is stunningly beautiful – and historic, since Richard the Lionheart was imprisoned in the now-ruined castle at Dürnstein.

The leading local grape is Grüner Veltliner, which at its most powerful produces a wine as rich and varied and scrummy as white Burgundy. Virtually all Veltliners from this part of the world are drinkable, and some are almost sublime. There are three grades, and the finest is, for some reason, called Smaragd, which sounds like a character in *The Lord of the Rings* but is, in fact, a local green lizard. I love Franz Hirtzberger's Smaragd, which I think is absolutely delectable, but which will cost you quite a bit.

JACKSON ESTATE GREY GHOST & GREEN LIP SAUVIGNON BLANC

Marlborough, New Zealand

WHITE ○○

Rich and full, and packed with scrummy fruit

It is often said in the wine world that while there might be many good Sauvignon Blancs, there are no great ones. I suspect there is at least one exception to this rule: the wines from Jackson Estate, in Marlborough, New Zealand.

The estate, now roughly 150 years old, has a glorious setting on the plain of the Wairu River. The wines are quite delectable – rich and full, and packed with scrummy fruit. They last over time, too, unlike many whites: you can go back ten years and find that the wines are just as crisp and fresh, but even more flavoursome and by now an iridescent golden colour.

All Jackson's wines are first-rate (they also make Pinot Noir and Chardonnay) but the very finest is Grey Ghost, a Sauvignon Blanc named after a mighty 140-metre gum tree planted outside the main house, where Jo Stichbury (she and her husband run the estate) can see it from the kitchen. The gum tree is known as 'the widow-maker' because to save water during dry seasons it sheds some of its huge branches – to the considerable peril of anyone sheltering underneath.

Grey Ghost has flavours of white peach, blackcurrant, toast and – this is not as silly as it sounds – stones. The Green Lip Sauvignon Blanc is also excellent, in spite of its off-putting name, which comes from the huge juicy mussels found in the sea near Marlborough. And it is delectable with all seafood.

DOMAINE JOSMEYER PINOT BLANC 'MISE DU PRINTEMPS'

Alsace, France

WHITE ○○─○○○

Alsace is a grossly neglected region. Crazy when you consider its wines are probably the most food-friendly of all (and the Alsaciens should know – they boast more Michelin-starred restaurants than anywhere else in France other than Paris).

The wines are punter-friendly too and accessible, in that unlike most of the rest of France they're sold under the name of their grape variety. And for those bored by the ubiquity of Sauvignon Blanc, Chardonnay or Cabernet Sauvignon, you won't see a wine here made from such grapes, however hard you look.

The best-known producers, such as Trimbach, Hugel, Zind-Humbrecht (see page 170) and Léon Beyer are names to conjure with, making extraordinary bone-dry to lusciously sweet wines of remarkable character. Josmeyer & Fils is firmly up there in my Alsace pantheon, too, a biodynamic/organic producer that makes exemplary Pinot Gris and fascinating blended whites, something of a rarity in Alsace where virtually all wines are single varietals.

My favourite Josmeyer wine is the utterly charming 'Mise du Printemps' made from 35-year-old Pinot Blanc vines. Pinot Blanc never gets star billing in Alsace; that's reserved for the mighty Riesling and spicy Gewurztraminer, but here in Josmeyer's hands Pinot Blanc is a star in its own right (although previous vintages have included some Pinot Auxerrois too). With succulent peaches and apples, hints of spring blossom, clean acidity and a delicately honeyed finish it makes for an utterly delightful glassful.

With succulent peaches and apples, hints of spring blossom, clean acidity and a delicately honeyed finish

KAIKEN ULTRA MALBEC

Mendoza, Argentina

RED ✪—✪✪

Ripe, warm, bursting with flavour but never quite overpowering

Argentina was late in coming to the attention of wine lovers. For a long time, the country meant little more than football, economic collapse, the Falklands War and steaks too big to fit on your plate. Since then Argentina has come on fast, and with its plantings of the Malbec grape variety is producing some stunning wines that particularly appeal to people who like a wine as beefy as the steaks and, without stretching a point too far, as shameless as Maradona. It's also perfect if you're looking for a change from blockbuster Aussie Shirazes, delicious though those can be.

Malbec is fundamentally the same variety as Auxerrois, used to make Cahors in France, but it's somewhat different, and in the hot Argentinian sun tends to produce a softer, much less tannic wine. At its best this really is superb – ripe, warm, bursting with flavour but never quite overpowering. You can detect more subtle notes here, of spices and flowers.

My choice of Kaiken is made by Aurelio Montes, probably the best known of all Chilean winemakers, who decided to cross the Andes (Mendoza, Argentina's main wine-producing area, is a short hop from Santiago) and aptly named his wine after a Patagonian goose that lives on both sides of the mountains. His Kaiken Ultra Malbec is pretty stunning. I was offered it at the celeb-haunted Ivy restaurant in London, where fellow guests included Melvyn Bragg and Ant & Dec (though it may have been Dec & Ant). The Kaiken, too, has a degree of stage presence.

I was offered it at the celeb-haunted Ivy
restaurant in London, where fellow guests
included Melvyn Bragg and Ant & Dec
(though it may have been Dec & Ant). The
Kaiken, too, has a degree of stage presence.

THE JUDGEMENT OF PARIS

In May 1976, an event took place that astounded the world of wine. It was held in Paris, capital of the country which, then and now, regards itself as the greatest, the *ne plus ultra*, of all wine-producing nations.

Indeed, some French people suspect fluids made outside their country are not merely inferior but scarcely merit the name 'wine', being little better than alcoholic grape juice. One British winemaker working in Bordeaux told me that when his colleagues visit UK wine stores, they are not just surprised to see the majority of non-French wines on sale, they are actually offended. Fortunately for the French economy, many winemakers have realized that, like it or not, these days they have to compete with wines from all over the world.

The 1976 event, inevitably known as 'The Judgement of Paris', was organized by a British wine expert working in the city, Stephen Spurrier. He recognized that many of the wines produced in California were now rivalling the best from Bordeaux. They might not have names that had resonated for centuries, but the combination of enterprising growers, investment money generated by a booming North American market, and

techniques discovered and refined by wine specialists working at the Davis campus of the University of California meant that many of the best were at least on a par with the great names of France.

Spurrier organized a blind tasting with nine French experts. To the astonishment of almost everyone (especially themselves), the experts agreed that the American wines were better. In fact, quite a lot better.

The resulting consternation was huge. It was as if the Japanese had beaten the finest Scottish single malts in a whisky tasting. The French rapidly regrouped. The wines, they pointed out, were only a few years old. The Californians aged quickly and had been sampled at their peak. Over the decades, the French wines would deepen and mature; their true class would outshine the New World and their unmatched greatness would be revealed once again to the world.

So 30 years later to the day, Stephen Spurrier organized another tasting, this time held simultaneously in Britain, usually regarded as a neutral venue, and in California itself. The tasting was again blind, though this time only two French experts agreed to take part. Most of the team who assembled at Berry Bros & Rudd, the historic wine merchants in London's St

James's, were British, and included some of the UK's leading experts: Jancis Robinson, Hugh Johnson and Michael Broadbent. I watched the tasting, and I have never seen such concentrated sipping, sluicing, slurping, swilling and spitting. They all wrote copious notes about each wine. This was as unlike a students' bring-a-bottle party as any such event could be.

The important fact was that the wines being tasted were not only from the same vineyards as those tried in 1976, but were the same vintages, which had had 30 more years to mature.

The result? Same as before. The Californians wiped the floor with the French, taking the first five places; the top French wine, Mouton-Rothschild 1970, came in sixth. Léoville-Las-Cases, one of the most celebrated (and expensive) Bordeaux reds, came ninth, saved from coming last by the only California wine not to shine. This was a 1969 Freemark Abbey, which had at some point collapsed in bottle so as to become almost undrinkable.

The French were deeply unhappy. Though it was clear that the Californian wines had outmatched their own even over several decades, some argued that a blind tasting was actually the worst way to try wines. Tasters, they claimed, could not know the history and traditions that came with each wine. Knowing what you are drinking is an essential part of the pleasure.

It was a pretty desperate plea, as anyone who tries the winner, Ridge California Monte Bello (see page 132), can tell.

Final 2006 Results

1   Ridge California Monte Bello 1971, California
2   Stag's Leap Wine Cellars 1973, California
3 = Heitz 1970, California;
     Mayacamas 1971, California
5   Clos du Val 1972, California
6   Ch Mouton-Rothschild 1970, Bordeaux
7   Ch Montrose 1970, Bordeaux
8   Ch Haut-Brion 1970, Bordeaux
9   Ch Léoville-Las-Cases 1971, Bordeaux
10   Freemark Abbey 1969, California

To the astonishment of almost everyone –
especially themselves – the gathered experts
agreed that the American wines were
better. In fact, quite a lot better.

CHÂTEAU LAFONT MENAUT
Pessac-Léognan, Bordeaux, France
WHITE ○○

Utterly delicious, a gorgeous summer wine that would make any picnic perfect

Entre-deux-Mers was one of those student wines we used to drink in the past. It didn't taste of anything very much, but then it didn't cost very much, either.

The name referred not to seas, but to two rivers: the Garonne and the Dordogne. I suspect that rather dreary fluid turned a generation of wine drinkers against dry white Bordeaux, which is a pity because these days there are some superb examples out there. I have chosen this Lafont Menaut, from the celebrated Pessac-Léognan region, partly because it tastes just delicious, but also for sentimental reasons. This particular estate was once owned by Montesquieu.

Most of the wines are a cunning blend of Sémillon and Sauvignon Blanc grapes. The Sauvignon brings its familiar flinty, hay, gooseberry and grass along to the party, while the Sémillon adds richness and the slightest touch of sweetness. (Sémillon is, of course, the grape that goes to make Sauternes and Barsac.) The net result is utterly delicious, a gorgeous summer wine that would make any picnic perfect. In one of the few wine ads I've ever seen that made you more inclined to drink the stuff, the white Bordeaux people showed two girls in floral dresses enjoying it in the sunshine. It's a 'girls in their summer frocks' wine – if you are one, or wish you were with one.

If you had a little more cash you might try the Château Doisy-Daëne sec from Barsac, which is made on an estate better known for its sweet wine, and which is fabulous.

LOUIS LATOUR
CORTON-CHARLEMAGNE
Burgundy, France
WHITE ✪✪✪✪

Rounded, smooth, almost too good to drink with food

A friend visiting us asked for a glass of white wine. 'Anything but Chardonnay,' she said. We offered white Burgundy. 'Now that would be lovely,' she replied. It's surprising how few people realize that white Burgundy isn't just made from Chardonnay – it is the epitome of the grape variety. In the New World they can make great Pinot Noirs, Sauvignon Blancs and Cabernets.

But few have come really close to matching a great white Burgundy: rich, creamy, concentrated, deep yet almost ethereal. Flavours seem to jostle for your attention, sometimes disappearing after the most fleeting appearance: hazelnuts, vanilla, honey, peaches and apricots. They are perfectly balanced, which is important, because while nobody ever said 'Waiter, bring me a perfectly balanced wine!' you'd quickly know if it was too acidic or too flabby.

During the phylloxera vine-louse epidemic of the 1880s, the Latour family bought the entire estate of Aloxe-Corton, where this wine is made just north of Beaune. It has been an incredible investment. They've always looked ahead, and are now cunningly buying into Beaujolais, currently the least-fashionable wine in France. This Corton-Charlemagne is majestic: rounded, smooth, almost too good to drink with food, as it would be hard to cook anything to match it. Can a wine be evanescent yet lingering? Apparently so.

DOMAINES LEFLAIVE MÂCON-VERZÉ
Maconnais, Burgundy, France
WHITE ✪✪✪

A lovely wine, perfect for celebrations

For a very long time, the wines of the Mâconnais, south of the greatest Burgundy-producing vineyards, were held in a sort of tentative, even grudging, esteem. To give you an idea of that, I've invented a particularly weird comparison: Harrow, the famous public school, and Harrow County School. The latter, a grammar, was an excellent school (Michael Portillo and Clive Anderson are old boys) but socially it wasn't up there with Churchill's alma mater, even if, individually, many of the grammar school pupils were as good as or better than, the fee-payers.

So there was a heavy symbolic resonance when Anne-Claude Leflaive of the great Burgundy family Leflaive, decided to buy land in Mâcon, to make wine with the grapes grown there and to sell it as Mâcon-Verzé – under the family name. It's as if a countess decided that the local grammar school was good enough for her son, provided he got some extra tutoring at home.

They don't actually make the wine in Mâcon. They press the grapes there, but then turn it into wine in Puligny-Montrachet, the famous Burgundy village which is home to the Leflaive clan. The result is gorgeous, even thrilling, combining the rich, round flavour of a great white Burgundy with a youthful zest. All at a price much lower than the equivalent quality from further north. Just in case, they switched the name on the label from 'Domaine Leflaive' to 'Domaines Leflaive'. Get it? It's as if the lad's CV read 'Education: Harrow' – then in tiny little letters, 'county school'.

Tortured analogies aside, this is a lovely wine, perfect for celebrations where you want to push the boat out, but not have to call the builders and cancel the new conservatory.

MADEIRA
Madeira, Portugal
FORTIFIED ✪✪

George Plantagenet, first Duke of Clarence, was not drowned in a butt of Malmsey wine, as the story has it; he was almost certainly executed in the Tower in 1478 for suspected disloyalty to his brother, Edward IV. A pity. It made a good story, which is why Shakespeare used it. Possibly it was used metaphorically and referred to a drink habit. We don't know.

Malmsey is one style of Madeira, which is not very fashionable now, but remains extremely delicious. (Older readers may recall the Flanders & Swann song, with its chorus 'Have some Madeira, m'dear', about a reprobate who uses the wine to seduce an innocent young woman.) The island of Madeira is southwest of Portugal, and was discovered (allegedly) in 1419, or possibly 1420, by João Gonçalves, known as 'the Squinter'. The whole island is only about 30 miles long, vertiginously steep, and at the time was covered in forest. The Squinter set fire to some trees in the hopes of clearing space, but succeeded in burning every scrap of vegetation on the island. It took about seven years for the fires to die down. In turn, this created a bare soil perfect for growing wine.

The wine that the Duke of Clarence did or did not drown in would not have been like the product on sale today. Madeira was on the trade routes west to the Americas and south to the Far East; barrels of wine fortified with brandy kept for the length of the voyage (it keeps more or less forever today) as well as being excellent ballast. It was hugely successful in the southern colonies of what became the United States of America. Now most Madeira is blended by the shippers, from a variety of years and a mixture of grape varieties.

Usually you would buy it as sweet, medium or dry. Prohibition almost killed off sales, but the growers survived and operate as a sort of collective. They sell their best wines under the names of Blandy and Cossart, though there are also vintage Madeiras, each from a single grape variety grown in a single year. With the exception of the cheap stuff, mainly sold in France to make *sauce madère*, it is almost all delicious and, these days, somewhat underappreciated.

The Squinter set fire to some trees in the hopes of clearing space, but succeeded in burning every scrap of vegetation on the island. It took about seven years for the fires to die down. In turn, this created a bare soil perfect for growing wine.

MENETOU-SALON BLANC

Loire Valley, France

WHITE ○○

Gorgeous and silky

Some years ago I had one of those wine epiphanies that delight the collector. We're like trainspotters seeing an old steam engine on an otherwise boring commuter line: it pleases us beyond reason.

We had been invited to stay with American friends who were celebrating their 20th wedding anniversary at a country hotel near Bourges. The hotel had its own wonderful garden and small collection of livestock. The food was simple but exquisite – just-picked baby vegetables in a light broth, their own chicken served in crisp pastry parcels. The wine they poured was equally simple but exquisite. It was the local white Menetou-Salon, of which I had never heard, but which turned out to be delectable. Menetou-Salon is a small *appellation* which adjoins Sancerre, a far more famous name that produces more than seven times as much wine.

The white is made from the same grape variety – Sauvignon Blanc – but I think it usually has more flavour. Those with finely tuned palates claim they can detect oranges, quince, blackcurrant, apples, mint, honey and spices, which strikes me, frankly, as an exaggeration. But there is no doubt that the wine is gorgeous and silky, and usually costs less than its more celebrated neighbour. Some Sancerre sells more on its name than its quality.

One of my favourites is made by Patricia Teiller, a beautiful woman who is the third generation of her family to make Menetou-Salon. She has almost perfect English, lives in a beautiful part of France, makes superb wine (her rosé is also wonderful) and has two lovely daughters. Who would not envy her?

Ask for Menetou-Salon in a restaurant and you will either confuse the wine waiter, or impress him mightily with your knowledge.

MITCHELL ESTATE RIESLING

Clare Valley, South Australia

WHITE ✪✪

Crisp and pungent

Clare Valley Riesling is made by Jane and Andrew Mitchell at their winery, Mitchell Estate, which has slatey soil very like the best in Germany. Riesling is probably the favourite grape variety of wine writers. This may be because, like rock critics, they like to demonstrate how distant they are from mere punters.

On the other hand, they may be right. Many people associate Riesling with those cheap wines we drank in our youth, such as the terrible Lutomer Riesling from the old Yugoslavia. This Australian version, however, is crisp and pungent, and has that ever-so-slightly oily feel which aficionados love.

ROBERT MONDAVI CARNEROS PINOT NOIR
Napa Valley, California, USA
RED ○○

Superb: rich, juicy, oozing with fruit and velvety flavour

I first met Robert Mondavi in early 1979, when he was already 63 years old. He was in the tasting room of his beautiful winery at Oakville, California, and he was sampling. Every morning he sampled 150 wines and every afternoon he sampled another 150. Even though he spat the whole lot out after swilling it round his mouth (I have never learned to spit; it seems such a waste, and in any case, you can't really appreciate a wine until it's gone down the gullet), there must have been enough alcohol absorbed by his body over the two sessions to send a lesser man reeling.

He was trying every one of his own wines, every day, at every stage of their production. There were many. Mondavi created wines from every leading grape variety and a few minor ones as well. He also tasted the competition, from all over the world, comparing Sancerres with his own Sauvignon Blanc, great Burgundies with his Pinot Noir and Chardonnay, Alsace wines with his own Gewurztraminer. But he also sampled the local wines because he was a man obsessed by creating the best, and he firmly believed that, in the end, California would match – and even overtake – the wines of the Old World.

Many believe that point has been reached. But Mondavi never thought it would be easy. I heard him speak at a dinner at the top of the World Trade Center – some years before it ceased to exist – and he invited us to try his Cabernet Sauvignon Reserve. We all made appreciative murmurs, and it was a very good wine indeed. But, he said, it wasn't yet there, it wasn't perfect; it still lacked the steely backbone of the French equivalent.

Mondavi set up his winery in 1966, having just left the family estate following a feud with his brother. In 1968 he created a Sauvignon Blanc – the grape was not well esteemed in the US at the time – and called it Fumé Blanc. The mild deception meant that the wine was a huge seller. In 1997 at the Grand European Jury Wine Tasting, his

Every morning he sampled 150 wines and every afternoon he sampled another 150. Even though he spat the whole lot out after swilling it round his mouth, there must have been enough alcohol absorbed by his body over the two sessions to send a lesser man reeling.

Chardonnay Reserve was voted best in the world. Mondavi's premium Los Carneros Pinot Noir is superb: rich, juicy, oozing with fruit and velvety flavour.

If you are ever in the Napa Valley, it's worth looking in. Mondavi himself is long gone, and the winery has been through various hands, but the building is stunning, you can taste the wines (though not 300 of them) and when I was there they weren't pressuring anyone to buy. A picnic of local meats and cheese, with a bottle of Mondavi's Cabernet Reserve or thrilling Pinot Noir Carneros, and a breeze off the hills cooling the California sun, is a memory that lingers.

Has a heady,
aromatic flavour

CHÂTEAU MONTUS
Madiran, France
RED ❂❂

Madiran is a wine that rewards patience. It comes from Gascony in the southwest corner of France, and in the days before wines were routinely moved thousands of miles around the world, it was a delightful surprise for pilgrims on their way to Santiago de Compostela.

Most Madiran is made from Tannat, another Cinderella grape that is rarely found outside the area – except in Latin America, where it has been grown very successfully in Uruguay of all places.

It is a very tannic grape, which means that in their youth the wines can be harsh and astringent – not something you will often find on the label. The growers usually add some Cabernet Sauvignon, itself fairly tannic, but less so and capable of softening the roughness of the Tannat.

When they get a bit of age, however, they become deliciously mellow and approachable – though never what you might call gentle – with a heady, aromatic flavour. Try, for example, a bottle of Montus. But because they have to be kept a few years to be really enjoyed, they cost more. And who is going to spend a substantial sum on a wine they've barely heard of? Some best-kept secrets are fated to remain best-kept.

WINE WAITERS

IT can be a terrifying moment. You're in an expensive restaurant. You are celebrating an important birthday, perhaps. Or making your number with a potential partner whom you know only slightly and whom you are desperately hoping to impress. Or maybe planning to close an important business deal. You've been fine with the food: you know what lobster and foie gras and oysters are, and you don't need to have *blanquette de veau* or a *timbale de legumes* explained. 'Thank you,' says the waiter, shutting his notebook, 'I'll send the sommelier over.'

The sommelier. The wine waiter. That fellow in a dicky bow with a sort of mutilated silver ashtray round his neck! (It's called a tastevin.) Now you really are on your own. Do you have the faintest idea what wine you want to drink? Have you a clue what will match your companion's fresh asparagus with pecorino cheese, or your sweetbreads in a hazelnut-flavoured reduction? Of course you don't. And suppose you decide not even to try bluffing, but throw yourself on his mercy? Won't he insist that a particularly expensive bottle is the only possible one to quaff with the combination of dishes you have ordered? What wine waiter anywhere, in the whole history of wine waiting, ever said 'Frankly, I'd go for a carafe of the house…'?

American novelist and wine writer Jay McInerney suggests saying, 'I was looking for an Austrian Riesling.' This has some advantages. First, it indicates that you are the kind of person who knows that Austrian Riesling exists, and are therefore sophisticated and knowledgeable. Secondly, it is unlikely to be on the list. If it is you may be snookered, especially as some Austrian Riesling is very expensive and might cost more than all the food. If the waiter replies, 'Austrian Riesling?' in a sneery sort of way, as if you had asked for a bottle of Thunderbird or Le Piat d'Or, you know that he is bluffing, and is possibly more ignorant about wine than you are. After he has gone, you can lean forward and say confidentially to your guest, 'I'm amazed he didn't know about Austrian Riesling. I was hoping they might have something from Wachau, but I don't think you'll find the Schloss Schickelgruber too disappointing.'

My problem with wine in restaurants is that it costs too much. As a wine writer, I feel a positive stab of pain when I see a wine which I know retails for, say, £6.50, on a menu priced at £20 or more.

Most restaurants have a mark-up of two-and-a-half to three times the retail price, which means at least four times the wholesale cost the restaurant has actually paid. This isn't simply greed: they have to find the rent and rates and wages somehow, and overcharging for wine is the traditional way of coping. But it still hurts. If I had £40 to spare, I would prefer to spend it on, say, three bottles of the same good wine purchased in an off-licence than the one bottle I'd get in a restaurant.

On the whole I would ignore the second cheapest. In many places it's the one with the biggest mark-up, or the one they bought too much of and need to lose quickly.

If you are on an expense account, that is not a problem. Ask the sommelier, and if he reports that the Château Talbot 2003 is drinking very well now, fork out the £100. Or, if you are a City slicker who can't quite believe he is still getting a bonus, the £6,000 for a bottle of Pétrus. But if you are paying with your own hard-earned money, you need a strategy. Here is mine.

Restaurants know that the second-cheapest wine on the list, red or white, is the one that goes fastest. Nobody wants to look a cheapskate. On the other hand, most people don't want to go berserk. That's why people let their eye stray down the list, just one place. On the whole I would ignore the second-cheapest.

At all costs – at least at your own cost – avoid the glamorous names. You will wind up paying for the glamour, not the flavour.

In many places it's the one with the biggest mark-up, or the one they bought too much of and need to lose quickly. Buy the house wine instead; in any half-decent restaurant that will be a half-decent wine. In some places, it is a very good wine.

Go for the New World. Wines from Chile and Argentina, for example, are likely to deliver more flavour for your buck than their French equivalents (though French country wines these days are often fabulous value). Don't buy Cloudy Bay from New Zealand – it's a big name, and it's monumentally overpriced. Indeed, don't buy any

wine merely because you've heard of it; that may be simply because they spend the money on advertising rather than improving the contents of the bottle. European wines from Spain, Italy and Germany are slow to move; they are also likely to be better value than France. At all costs – at least at your own cost – avoid the glamorous names.
You will wind up paying for the glamour, not the flavour.

Be confident. You are not trying to impress the wine waiter. You don't hope to go to bed with him later that night, and you don't plan to go into business with him, either. Be courteous, listen to what he has to say, but make your own mind up. Never be afraid to look cheap. If a cheaper wine is on the wine list in a good restaurant, it should be a good wine. If it isn't a good wine, it's a poor restaurant and doesn't deserve your custom. Of course, if you see any of the wines in this book, snap them up immediately.

Here's another tip. When the waiter keeps scurrying round to top up your glass, it could be that he is simply providing excellent and attentive service. Or it could be that he hopes you'll drink the first bottle quickly and will need a second one soon. Or it might be both. But if you don't want that second bottle, and equally don't want to be wineless at the end of the meal, simply smile politely and say, 'Thank you so much, but we'll pour it ourselves.' You'll find they take the hint.

MULDERBOSCH FAITHFUL HOUND
Stellenbosch, South Africa
RED ○○

A complex wine and deeply satisfying

When Larry Jacobs and Mike Dobrovic took over the Mulderbosch estate in Stellenbosch, near Cape Town, they were intrigued by an old reddish mongrel dog that seemed to be keeping wait for something or for someone. It would help around the vineyard, watching for strangers, then every night it would return to sleep under the same tree. They called the dog the Faithful Hound, and decided to name their Bordeaux style of red wine after him and put him on the label. The wine has become a huge international hit, and in my view is better value than most real Bordeaux at the same price.

Faithful Hound is around 40 per cent Merlot and slightly less Cabernet Sauvignon, which means it's softer than, say, most Médocs. It's easy (see elsewhere in this book) to make fun of wine writers and the way they seem to detect flavours hidden from those of us with less finely attuned palates. On the other hand, wine needs to be described somehow, and here are some of the tastes detected in Faithful Hound: spices, plums, smoke, cherries, blackcurrants, forest-floor fruits, nutmeg, coffee, mulberries, toast, liquorice, tobacco and herbs. In other words, this is a complex wine and deeply satisfying.

Later Jacobs and Dobrovic discovered that the dog's name was *Boes*, the Boer word for 'bushy'. Its owner had been a vineyard employee called Nimrod, who died in a truck accident. The hound never stopped waiting for his master to return, until he himself died.

They were intrigued by an old reddish
mongrel dog that seemed to be keeping
wait for something or for someone. It would
help around the vineyard, watching for strangers,
then every night it would return to sleep
under the same tree. They called
the dog the Faithful Hound.

2000
Chateau Musar
★
GASTON HOCHAR
WINE OF LEBANON · BEKAA VALLEY

Like a fine claret, with heady and exotic flavours

CHATEAU MUSAR
Bekaa Valley, Lebanon
RED & WHITE ✪✪—✪✪✪

I met Serge Hochar and his brother Ronald early in the millennium. It is Serge who makes the fabled Chateau Musar, and Ronald, a man with a gleam in his eye, who does the accounts and the marketing. We were in Christopher's restaurant in Covent Garden, London, sampling several of the nine different wines the brothers export, along with the restaurateur, Christopher Gilmour. At one point Ronald excused himself, but instead of heading for the bathroom, he marched into the kitchen. 'He can't go there!' exclaimed Christopher. 'I think,' said Serge, in his faultless, heavily French-accented English, 'that he might be looking for our beautiful waitress…' Seconds later Ronald re-appeared, unbowed, but with a slight smile.

I mention this only because the Hochar brothers have always lived close to the edge. Musar was founded by their father, Gaston, in the Lebanese town of Ghazir. During the Second World War, he met the Irish winemaker Ronald Barton, of Châteaux Langoa and Léoville-Barton, who was stationed in Lebanon, and after whom the younger brother was named. Barton inspired in Gaston a passion for fine winemaking, though for decades virtually all their production was sold at home. Then, in 1979, Musar created a sensation at the Bristol Wine Fair and the name of the wine spread around the world. Nowadays 85 per cent of its production is sold abroad. (Some people snobbishly wondered how a fine wine could come from Lebanon, but then the Levant is the cradle of wine, having been made there as early as 6,000 BC.)

The civil war in Lebanon created appalling problems for the brothers. Their grapes are grown in the Bekaa Valley, 50 miles from Ghazir, and during the war the road down which they travelled was lined with snipers, roadblocks, checkpoints and gun-toting gangsters demanding money. One time the Syrians were shelling the neighbourhood where the Hochars live – they are Maronite Christians, whose family have lived in Lebanon for a thousand years. Family and friends begged Serge to take cover. But he refused; instead he took a bottle of the 1972 and poured it into one giant glass. Over the 12 hours the shelling continued, he sipped the wine, noting carefully how it changed hour by hour through exposure to the air.

Somehow they managed to make wine in every year but two – 1976 and 1984 – and the 1983, created at the height of the fighting, is one of their very finest vintages, rivalling the incredible 1988.

There are three different levels each of red, white and rosé wine, though it is the leading red wine that has made Musar world famous. It's like a fine claret (Cabernet Sauvignon is the main grape variety), though with heady and exotic flavours imparted by Cinsault and Carignan.

The white is harder to come by, but it's worth seeking out: it is made from a blend of two local grape varieties, probably the ancestors of Chardonnay and Sémillon, and to my mind tastes a little like liquid tarte tatin, with apples, spices and cream. Some people suggest that Musar is now past its best – other Lebanese winemakers are also coming up with fine results – but I think it is still the finest, a monument to dedication and resilience.

Family and friends begged Serge to take cover. But he refused; instead he took a bottle of the 1972 and poured it into one giant glass. Over the 12 hours the shelling continued, he sipped the wine, noting carefully how it changed hour by hour through exposure to the air.

QUINTA DO NOVAL RED
Douro Valley, Portugal
RED ✪✪✪–✪✪✪✪

Oodles of finesse

The Douro Valley in northern Portugal is one of the oldest of all wine producing areas. It also happens, in a way, to be one of the newest. Long famous for its vintage and tawny ports (it was the first wine region in the world to be officially demarcated in 1756), the Douro has recently created quite a stir with its full-throttled and expressive red table wines.

Of course they always did make wine here. It was the British who started fortifying Douro wines with brandy in order that they would survive the voyage home. As João Nicolau de Almeida, MD of Ramos Pinto, one of the first to produce and market the new table wines, once told me, "We're just looking for something that we lost. We're simply waking from a long sleep and rediscovering our past."

Established port producers such as Quinta do Noval, Quinta de la Rosa, Real Companhia Velha, Ramos Pinto and Symington Family Estates as well as new producers such as Quinta do Poeira and loose collaborations such as Lavradores de Feitoria and the quintet of quintas which comprises the so-called Douro Boys (Quinta do Vale Meão, Quinta do Crasto, Quinta Vale Dona Maria, Quinta do Vallado and Niepoort) all produce superb, deep, dark and intense wines from the vertiginous terraces along the Douro.

Quinta do Noval, in the same AXA Millésimes stable as such blue chip estates as Château Pichon Baron in Pauillac (see page 120), Château Suduiraut in Sauternes, Disznókö in Hungary and Domaine de l'Arlot in Burgundy, is my pick of the bunch.

AXA Millésimes's head, Christian Seely, arrived at an ailing Noval in 1993 as its newly appointed MD. He completely turned around the estate's fortunes, putting it firmly back at the forefront of port producers. He also instigated the production of unfortified red table wine, made with the same varieties that go to make port, with its first vintage in 2004.

The current vintage – 2012 – is an awesome beauty: rich, intense, concentrated, powerful, tannic with – as everyone who tastes it agrees – oodles of finesse. Do try some Douro reds because they're unlike anything made anywhere else. If you only try one, try Quinta do Noval.

ORNELLAIA
Bolgheri, Tuscany, Italy
RED ✪✪—✪✪✪✪

A beguiling blend of flavours which develop over the hours

When Ludovico Antinori, a member of one of Italy's best-known wine families, wanted to set up his own estate, he thought of going to California, where he had had winemaking experience. He was persuaded, however, to stay in Tuscany – specifically in Maremma, a marshy area by the coast, which until then had been thought good for nothing except as sparse grazing for a few lonely cattle. It was a bold move. Tuscan winemaking was in crisis, with many small growers looking to sell off their properties.

Antinori's choice of terrain seemed strange, but turned out to be perfect. The breezes off the sea tempered the heat of summer, and the hills behind protected the area from the cold winter winds that can be damaging further inland. The land was perfect not just for Sangiovese, the grape variety that normally goes into Tuscan wine, but for Cabernet Sauvignon, Merlot and other varieties normally associated with Bordeaux. In short, Antinori was going to produce a knock-off claret, but an imitation that would be better than all but a handful of the originals, a fake Rolex that kept better time than a real Rolex. Now his flagship wine, Ornellaia, is rated one of the world's great reds, and can fetch hundreds of pounds a bottle.

It is magnificent, full and rich and velvety, with a zest and fruitiness few clarets can match. It also has a beguiling blend of flavours that develop over the hours after a bottle has been opened: cedar, blackcurrant, mint, chocolate and smoke – some of these seem to come and go, to linger for a short while, then disappear to make way for others. Even the most mature, elderly bottles have kept a certain youthful vigour, like a sprightly grandfather who can still dance.

If you can't afford the Ornellaia, you can buy for far less the second wine, Le Serre Nuove. When it's been a great year for Cabernet Sauvignon, they put more of that into the main wine; the same when it's Merlot that has done well. And the vines are younger. But it is still a delectable, succulent wine.

There have been several owners. Mondavi, the great California grower, bought the estate in 1997, then five years later sold half of it to Frescobaldi, who acquired the rest in 2005. But the winemaking personnel has stayed unchanged, and Ornellaia is a rare example of a wine that's been sold to a big conglomerate but has kept its quality and character.

Even the most mature, elderly bottles have kept a certain youthful vigour, like a sprightly grandfather who can still dance.

CHÂTEAU PAVIE
Saint-Émilion, Bordeaux, France
RED ✪✪✪✪✪

A lovely mellow, cedary Saint-Émilion, soft but with a terrific underlying power

This is another old favourite of mine, but greatly changed. I prefer the old style, but that's a bit like saying you liked the old bullfrog-shaped Citroën rather than the spanking new Xsara. It's a matter of affection and memory.

But first a word about Robert Parker, the sage of Maryland. He is overwhelmingly the most important and influential wine writer in the world, bar nobody at all, anywhere. Others, many in Britain, have strong opinions, too, but the British market counts for much less. What any grower ambitious for profits wants to do is to please Parker.

He does, it is said, have a quite phenomenal palate and an astounding ability to recall the taste of wine, in the way that some people can recite whole Shakespeare plays from memory. In his trade it is extremely useful. 'This is, I think, a Château Cauchemar, younger but if anything more profound than the 1995 I tasted at the vineyard…' His secret is his grading system, which on the surface removes the vagaries of chance for anxious purchasers. He gives 50–100 points for every wine he tries, or in reality 80–100, since he'd never trouble the typesetters with a wine that was much below that. In other words, if you're in the shop and a wine is labelled with '93 Parker points' you might well think it's better than one that has only 91. Whether you'll like it more is a different matter. But you can tell your friends 'This is a Parker 93' and at least they'll have someone else to blame if they don't like it.

I heard Robert Parker speak some years ago at a dinner in the Banqueting Hall in Whitehall, London, the room from which Charles I was taken to be executed. The dinner was to show off different vintages of four superb red Bordeaux wines. Mr Parker began by describing the climatic conditions in the Médoc in the year 1900, plus the timing and length of each spell of sun and rain, before moving on to 1901 and so on, and on. I asked my neighbour to wake me when we got to the Occupation. By the time the speaker had reached the 1960s, I suspect many of his audience would have happily swapped places with King Charles.

It's fair to say that there has long been tension between Parker and his British equivalents. The great Michael Broadbent of Christie's once described attending a dinner given by one of his own clients in San Francisco. 'All the wines had been scored 100 by Parker, and I could see why. Of course, they were all quite undrinkable...' he said, to much laughter. At Corney & Barrow, staff members are fined if they are overheard mentioning his name.

The British complaint is that Parker loves 'fruit bombs': powerful, over-flavoured, over-extracted (too much stuff squeezed out of the grape) wines. And because he rates them highly, they sell much better in the US, and French growers in particular are inclined to 'Parkerize' their wines, losing – it is said – subtlety, finesse, grace and the elusive terroir. For his part he believes – and these are my own words – that British wine writers are stuck-in-the-mud, self-important, too conservative and, in the English demotic, up themselves.

Things came to a head in 2004 in a row over Château Pavie. This is a wine which the Army & Navy Stores used to bottle itself and sell under its own label in the mid-1970s for £2 a half.

Now it's nearer £200 for a full bottle. It was, I used to think, a lovely mellow, cedary Saint-Émilion, soft but with a terrific underlying power. In 1998 the estate was bought by Gérard Perse, who promptly, if the word means anything, Parkerized the product. Parker duly thought it was terrific. Jancis Robinson, in the British corner, rated the 2003 at only 12 points out of 20 – a dreadfully low score for a wine as expensive and prestigious as this.

Parker and Perse accused her of bad faith, saying she had it in for Perse's wines. She replied that she had disliked it at a blind tasting. They said that she must have known it was Pavie because Pavie is sold in a distinctively shaped bottle. She riposted that it had come as a cask sample in an ordinary bottle so she couldn't possibly have known. And so on.

The battle, ended by a truce, was about more than one wine – it was about New World versus Old, tradition versus innovation, and about changing tastes in wine. But I still prefer the old. If you are lucky enough to stumble across a pre-1998 bottle of Pavie, buy it. Or, if necessary, acquire it by underhand means. ('What? You've still got this dusty old thing? Tell you what, I'll swap it for two bottles of Le Piat d'Or.')

His secret is his grading system, which on the surface removes the vagaries of chance for anxious purchasers. He gives 50–100 points for every wine he tries, or in reality 80–100, since he'd never trouble the typesetters with a wine that was much below that.

PESQUERA CRIANZA
Ribera del Duero, Spain
RED ✪✪–✪✪✪

Rich, warm,
velvety, heady
and perfumed

This is a great wine from northern Spain. (*Crianza* merely means 'aged', in the case of reds, for at least two years, including a minimum of 12 months in oak barrels.) It is made by Alejandro Fernández from the Tempranillo grape variety, and it is rich, warm, velvety, heady and perfumed.

It doesn't have too much oak; instead, it is just enough to give it *gravitas* – and tastes of blackberries and blackcurrants, among other nice things. If I told you that some of its fans also thought that it had notes of 'iodine', 'sappy cling', 'road tar', and 'cow sheds', that shouldn't put you off. No, really.

CHÂTEAU PÉTRUS
Pomerol, Bordeaux, France
RED ✪✪✪✪✪

Maybe this should be listed as a wine not to try before you die. Because you can't afford it, and even if you could, you'd be better off giving all the money to the orphans' home. It's what I call a Simon Cowell wine, bought by people who have far more money than taste, who buy stuff mainly to impress other multimillionaires with how rich they are.

A friend's daughter worked as a chalet girl in Chamonix and reported seeing Russian oligarchs order Pétrus, then stiffen it with vodka. Last time I looked, Berry Bros & Rudd was selling a bottle of 1990 for £4,665.

It took time for Pétrus to gain its extraordinary prestige. Until the war, it was regarded as one of the better wines of Pomerol, the small Bordeaux region near Saint-Émilion, but not the best. There is no great château, only a modest two-storey house decorated by a statuette of St Peter carrying a giant key to the pearly gates.

It was only after 1945 that the wine's reputation began to grow. In 1947 it was served at the wedding of Princess Elizabeth and Philip Mountbatten. In 1960 it took off among the American rich when it was featured at New York's most fashionable restaurant, Le Pavillon. In 2004, owner Jean-François Moueix was asked permission for Pétrus to be featured in the popular and influential film *Sideways*. A bottle was to be the prized possession of the leading character, an obsessive wine-lover. Moueix didn't care for the script, so the writers picked a 1961 Cheval Blanc instead, which the wine-lover drinks from a plastic cup, in a diner, accompanied by fried onion rings. At one stage he expresses contempt for the Merlot grape, a puzzling remark that had much influence in American wine-drinking circles. In fact, Pétrus is made entirely from Merlot, except very occasionally when a dash of Cabernet Franc is added. Cheval Blanc is generally half Cabernet Franc.

I finally got to drink Pétrus in 2010, aptly enough in Hatton Garden, the heart of London's diamond quarter. It was ten years old, admittedly far too young to be at its best, and while I enjoyed it, it didn't taste like some kind of ambrosia. But the bottle came from a case priced at £34,000 and the slug I poured myself would have cost around £200. I just wanted to taste what that value of wine was like. The temptation to say, very loudly, 'Through the teeth and round the gums, look out stomach, here it comes!' was very great, but resisted. Instead I sipped it reverentially. And Pétrus wasn't even the most expensive wine at the tasting. Le Pin cost slightly more.

WINE LABELS

It's surprising how many winemakers just don't realize how important their label is. Imagine you're in an off-licence, looking for something to serve your dinner guests, or to enjoy with a Chinese takeaway. You're faced with literally hundreds of different bottles. What's the first thing you look for, seeking guidance? The label, of course.

And what do you see? Maybe a French wine that tells you where it comes from, but nothing about what it tastes like. Or a German wine, covered in old-fashioned Gothic blackletter writing, almost illegible to our eyes, with a few lengthy German words in and around the label. Is it sweet or dry? Floral or oily? How can you tell?

The New World wines are a little more helpful. As well as giving you the brand name, they almost always tell you the grape variety, and where the wine is made.

That can be a help. A Syrah, for example, is likely to go well with a roast or even a curry. A Sauvignon Blanc would be great with fish or white meat. So that's a start. But little more. No wonder many people give up in despair, and either choose a wine they've liked in the past, or just go to the guy behind the counter and say, 'I want to spend around £6 or £7 and it's to go with coq au vin.'

And many labels are, frankly, unattractive. I often meet merchants who say to winemakers, 'Look, we could sell a lot more if you produced an appealing label,' only to be told, 'My customers know that what counts is what's inside the bottle.'

That sounds as if it ought to be true, but it isn't. For one thing, people frequently buy wine to serve to their friends. They don't want to seem tight-fisted, so they don't want a wine that looks cheap. Naturally the fact that a French wine has a picture of a crumbling château on the bottle doesn't make it taste nice, but it does look nice. A simple handwritten line of script may suggest a lack of pretension, a decent, rustic honesty, but it also implies the bottom end of the market. 'Fat Bastard' – believe it or not, a French wine – would be great for a student party, but would you want to serve it with a meal someone had spent hours lovingly preparing?

So what do you look for? Alcohol level will always appear somewhere on the bottle. To creep in under EU regulations, 14.5 per cent alcohol by volume is the maximum you're likely to see. Sometimes that really means 15 per cent, but a whole load of regulations kick in at that point, so winemakers try to avoid reaching it. Some German wines are quite low in alcohol, as weak as, say, nine per cent. These are often good for people who want to enjoy the taste and refreshing qualities of wine, but are driving or pregnant. EU regulations have to state if a wine 'contains sulfites', which almost all do – these are a natural by-product of the winemaking process, but they can affect some people adversely.

From here on you can be on your own. A French wine will tell you what region it is from, and in most cases that is assumed to be enough. If you want to know the grape, tough – you're supposed to know already. But increasingly, because of international pressure, more French winemakers are allowed to put the name of the grape on the label, and that's a huge help.

Burgundy is a mass of confusing different labels, indicating who grew the grapes, who made them into wine, and who sold them. You have to go by price, experience and personal choice. Red Bordeaux, or claret, is somewhat easier. The very finest wines are divided into five crus, or growths, and the first growths command frightening prices. Some, such as the nominally third growth Château Palmer, should in most people's view be near the very top, which is why it costs around £200 a bottle. Some of the best and priciest wines come from satellite regions, such as Saint-Émilion and Pomerol. You are unlikely to see those in your local supermarket.

Is there a way through this bewildering maze that doesn't involve doing a serious wine course?

No. You need to take advice, decide what you want to spend, and go back to a wine if you like it enough to buy it again. And get top tips from merchants and from friends. Here's a tip from me. If the label says Grand Vin de Bordeaux it means nothing at all except that the maker wants you to think that it's a great Bordeaux wine. Maybe it is. Just as likely, it isn't.

And not every red wine ages well. All but the best Beaujolais should be drunk when it's fresh. Other wines fade with age, and acquire a sort of dusty taste. On the other hand, some will last for an astonishingly long time.

That gives you some idea of how complicated it all is. Then, to make matters worse, there's the vintage, or date. What this means depends entirely on the wine. With a fine Bordeaux or Burgundy, the date can be very helpful. Some years were good, some not so good. Some were massively hyped at the time but have fallen back. Others seemed disappointing when they came out, but have improved unexpectedly. And the fact that it was a 'good year' doesn't mean it was good for everyone. Prices often reflect the varying quality, but not always.

And not every red wine ages well. All but the best Beaujolais should be drunk when it's fresh. Other wines fade with age, and acquire a sort of dusty taste. On the other hand, some will last for an astonishingly long time. I once drank a Volnay – red Burgundy – that was 75 years old and was still perfectly pleasant. I've had far more recent wines that had gone thin, pale and wan.

Most white wines should be drunk young. But Sauternes and Barsac last well, becoming lustrously golden, right until they become a deep orange, when they too start to lose it. Great white Burgundies can last for years – if you're lucky. I've had some ghastly oxidized wines that stank of drains.

Luckily, since turnover is so fast, most merchants and supermarkets only sell wine that is still in reasonable nick. Just don't imagine you'll learn very much from the date. A southern hemisphere wine dated with the year we're still in would have been made in their autumn, our spring, and can be fresh, lively and delicious. An aged wine might look dignified, but can taste nasty and sour.

There is always the back label. Not all wines have one, but when they do it is usually in English, or at least bilingual, on wines sold in Britain. Basically it's an advert. 'This wine is made from the finest selected Tempranillo grapes grown in the sun-dappled vineyards of the Cojones Mountains. The grapes are lovingly harvested, before being fermented and matured in oak barrels to draw out the richness of their profound and complex flavours. A wine to enjoy with any number of foods, including foie gras, fillet steak, game and casseroles. Contains sulfites.'

Sometimes they go berserk. 'The legend is told of the maiden Astrid, daughter of a cruel nobleman, who fell in love with a handsome young farmhand ... after she died her soul was said to haunt the vineyards where we grow our hand-selected Chardonnay grapes.'

That's all about as useful as an insurance commercial when you're trying to buy insurance, but at least it might give you some vague idea of what food to team it with. On the whole, I wouldn't drink Syrah with smoked salmon, or Pinot Grigio with venison. So the back label can help you avoid those and similar mistakes – unless it's only rabbiting on about local legends.

Italian wines

There are some words that can help to guide you. On an Italian wine, classico usually means 'better than average'. Generally it will indicate a wine made by a specific vigneron who attaches his or her name or the name of the estate to the bottle. It isn't just heaved from a hopper into the local co-op. Soave Classico, or Chianti Classico, can be really delicious and quite a revelation. Some Italian labels help by telling you the grape variety, but since around 2,000 different grapes are grown in Italy, that help goes only so far.

Spanish wines

In Spain you may get help and you may not. Albariño is a grape variety that makes lovely, aromatic whites. But Rioja and Ribera del Duero probably won't tell you the grape variety. You have to know that Rioja will probably taste oaky with vanilla flavours; Ribera del Duero might be fuller in flavour.

German wines

Let's not go there. I have tried to give a rough idea of what to look for in the piece on German wine (page 61), but like those scholars who go mad studying the Talmud for the whole of their lives, there are probably people who have lost their reason trying to master the intricacies of German wine.

My main advice would be to avoid the generics (for whose poor quality the German industry is still paying the price), such as Blue Nun, and go for something made by a particular person in a particular place. 'Schickelgruber/ Johannes Bratwurst/Riesling Kabinett tells you that this is a medium- to high-quality wine made by Johannes Bratwurst in or near the village of Schickelgrub. It's a fairly dry Riesling.

Australian wines

Occasionally the origin will help. Margaret River, Barossa, Clare Valley all produce good wines – very good wines. But so do other regions. Vintages count for less in the New World, where one year tends to be much like another. On the other hand, the finer wines will have benefitted from years in the bottle or cask.

New Zealand wines

The main areas include Marlborough, Martinborough, Hawke's Bay, and Central Otago. But the fact that the wine comes from one of those areas doesn't prove anything at all. New Zealand wines cost, on average, more than any other country's – this is because they make no plonk, and so on the whole are reliable. Though most experts now reckon the most famous of all, Cloudy Bay, is now not what it was and is overpriced.

USA wines

Even when the dollar was low, these tended to be pricey. Americans are proud of their wine, and are prepared to pay a premium price to get it. I recall sampling a particularly nice Cabernet at a tasting given by the growers themselves. How much, I asked, did it cost? 'That would be 80 of your English pounds,' the man said. 'Amazing value for a case!' I replied. 'No, a bottle,' he said. Again, apart from the modest help offered by the region – Napa Valley, Russian River, Oregon, etc – you simply have to rely on the producers' names and the grape variety to give you even a hint of the quality within.

The complexity of wine labelling is, no doubt, one reason why people often give up experimenting and quickly settle on one or two wines they enjoy and find reliable. That's a shame. But there are ways through the problem.

Price can be a guide. Generally the classic French regions are overpriced on the grounds that, say, 'If it's a Burgundy, it must be good'. True, up to a point. But the fact is that a £10 Malbec from Argentina will probably be smoother, fuller and less sharp than a £6 bottle. An £11 Chardonnay from Margaret River in Australia will be much more exciting than a £5.50 wine from one of the big companies that make and export millions of litres. In my view, a £12 wine from southern France is likely to be far better value than any Bordeaux at the same price.

And finally, as I always say, take advice. If you're lucky enough to have a local independent merchant, cultivate him. Okay, you may wind up at the supermarket or the excellent Majestic Wine Warehouse if you're giving a party for 60 people, much as your local guy wishes you didn't. But the independents usually know and love their wines, take real pride in finding those that are interesting and good value, and are delighted to discuss them with you.

A lot of companies also offer a mail-order service. As I point out elsewhere, the apparently astounding bargains offered by some are rarely quite what they seem; the prices on which the savings are based are invented by the dealer himself. (It's as if John Grisham announced that his latest paperback was 'worth' £15, so that £6.99 was an amazing discount.)

But companies such as Corney & Barrow, The Wine Company of Colchester, Yapp Bros, Adnams of Southwold, Suffolk, Avery's of Bristol, Wrightson Wines in Yorkshire, Private Cellar in East Anglia, Swig of West London, Tanner's in Shrewsbury, and many others all offer a nationwide service. FromVineyardsDirect cuts out the middleman by going straight to the growers. These firms are staffed by knowledgeable people who will be happy to help with your choice.

And, of course, I like to think you can rely on The Spectator. We almost always offer generous discounts, and invariably free delivery. And, again, you don't need to worry about the label – that's all done for you.

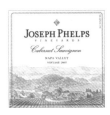

JOSEPH PHELPS
CABERNET SAUVIGNON
Napa Valley, California, USA

RED ✪✪✪

A classic Bordeaux blend, with just a little bit of Merlot to add a touch of softness

A visit to the Haut-Médoc and a visit to the Napa Valley could hardly be more different. The leading region of Bordeaux is closed, buttoned up. The great and famous names are proclaimed by the side of the road, but this is scarcely an invitation. Don't go to Château Margaux, rattle the gates and hope to be let in for a tasting. The *vignerons* of this region are cool, graceful but reserved.

Once you are in, it is a different story. If you come with an introduction or, even better, with someone they know, they will be warm and welcoming. A former wine writer friend of mine tells of going with a colleague to dinner at Château Lafite-Rothschild, where their eponymous host insisted on opening bottles made in both the years of their birth.

But most of us, most of the time, can't do that. If you drive round the area (the Médoc is scenically rather dull, though the hill towns of, say, Saint-Émilion are more attractive), you might see the occasional sign *Vente et Dégustation* (Tasting and Sales), but they will be on properties you have probably never heard of. The owners are unlikely to want to waste much time showing you round the place, and even if they do – well, unless you're a wine anorak, once you've seen one bottling plant, you've seen them all. If you like the wine, it might well be at a reasonable price – though the Bordelais follow the markets very carefully, and you can easily pay more in a shop a few miles from where the wine is made than in a British off-licence, where news of price rises has taken longer to filter back.

If you really would like to see round a winery it can be done – best to go to one of the Syndicats Viticoles in the small towns – Saint-Émilion, Lalande de Pomerol, Libourne, and so forth, and just ask what is available. But don't expect a guided tour of Château Pétrus.

This is why the contrast with the Napa Valley is so great. For one thing, Napa is scenically quite splendid. And the Americans quickly embraced the notion of wine tourism. Most Californian properties allow visitors in, unannounced, and usually free – though, if there is a charge it is modest, and almost invariably refunded if you buy wine. Some of the vineyards are spectacular; it's worth visiting Mondavi for the architecture alone, though the tour is helpful and informative, and there is a very wide choice of excellent wines available for tasting. The Chandon estate offers sparkling wine and nibbles in a gorgeous garden setting. At Sterling, the property is dominated by a crag to which you ascend by cable car, though their wines are not so thrilling. The wineries that are unlikely to let you in are those which make tiny quantities sold to people on long waiting lists. They don't need the public; they have their names and reputations. If the rest are Madame Tussauds for the masses, these are the Queen's Picture Gallery.

One of my favourite Napa wines is made by Joseph Phelps. Their Cabernet Sauvignon is a recreation of a classic Bordeaux blend, including just a little bit of Merlot to add a touch of softness. Now and again, I like to quote winemakers on their own wine, if only to communicate the enthusiasm they probably quite genuinely feel. 'A rich bouquet of cinnamon, spice, liquorice, graphite and caramel are followed by integrated layers of cherry, currant, fresh cream, and balanced sweet tannin…' And, as it happens, that is all perfectly true, though I'm not so sure about the graphite. If they were British, I'd assume they were saying it puts lead in your pencil.

Rich and dark, packed with fruity flavours, and ready to keep for a very long time

CHÂTEAU PICHON-LONGUEVILLE BARON

Pauillac, Bordeaux, France

RED ✪✪✪✪

I like this wine for the perfectly good reason that it is made by an Englishman, Christian Seely. Christian is one of the most charming people you will ever meet, and of course his nationality means that he can stand to one side of the great complicated feuds and rivalries that extend like fissures in the rock throughout Bordeaux.

One of the most intense was between the two neighbouring Rothschilds, Elie of Château Lafite-Rothschild, and Philippe of Château Mouton-Rothschild. Traditionally, the two felt obliged to serve each other's wines at important meals. Once Philippe offered an inferior Lafite with a curried dish, before serving a magnificent Mouton '59 with the cheese. The story was denied, but the wine writer Nicholas Faith, who tells it in his book *The Winemasters*, had a copy of the menu.

At a dinner we asked Christian if his French colleagues were prepared to forgive him for being English. 'They have forgiven me,' he said, 'but they will not let me forget it.' Just as the Japanese believe that no non-Japanese person can master chopsticks – even though they took that custom from the Chinese – so, in spite of the evidence of their own eyes, do the French not quite believe a non-French person can make any kind of real wine, even though their country is full of foreigners doing exactly that.

Pichon Baron is a 'second growth' or *deuxième cru*, which puts it in the rank just behind the top five wines, or first growths, many of which can command prices four or more times as high as those immediately below. These ratings are enshrined in the great classification of 1855, which preserved almost all Bordeaux properties in a virtually unchanging, marmoreal order. (It was not until 1973 that Baron Philippe managed to get Mouton inserted into the top rank, where it richly deserved to be.) Keeping the rankings almost unchanged for more than a century and a half is not quite as ludicrous as it might seem, since the basic soil and geographical situations remain the same.

On the other hand, owners do come and go, châteaux are well run or badly run, get the investment they need or are starved of cash. Pichon Baron was one that had been left behind. However, in 1987 a new winemaker, Jean-Michel Cazes, arrived, and with a massive investment by the new owner, the giant French insurance group AXA, he turned the property into a 'super-second', one of the second growths that rival – and almost match – the firsts.

It is a lovely wine, rich and dark, packed with fruity flavours, and ready to keep for a very long time. But it costs only a small proportion of the Latours, Lafites and Moutons. And in a way you are buying a top-class British wine.

Deep, dark, packed
with winter fruits

PINOTAGE
Stellenbosch, South Africa
RED ✪✪

There are one or two places where they grow Pinotage
outside South Africa, but it's not exactly making anyone's
fortune. Pinotage is a cross between Pinot Noir, which is
the grape in red Burgundy and fine wines in New Zealand,
Oregon and several other places, and Cinsault, a high-
producing grape known in South Africa as Hermitage,
hence the hybrid name (from 'Pinot' plus 'tage'). For many
years Pinotage was famous for being muddy. This does not
sound very appealing, and to many drinkers it wasn't – or
at least not for more than a single bottle. Or a single sip. It
was a bit like drinking retsina on holiday in Greece. You
might enjoy it to wash down the moussaka and *dolmades* in
a sun-drenched beachside *taverna*, but you'd hardly be likely
to seek it out when you got home. For that reason around
two-thirds of South Africa's Pinotage vines were uprooted to
make space for more popular varieties.

However, some people – a minority, to be sure – liked
the muddiness. Anthony Mitchell of El Vino's once told
me that he had a customer who complained about his
Pinotage. 'Haven't you got anything muddier?' he asked,
in the manner of someone in a grubby raincoat asking for
something stronger in a Soho porn store.

Actually some other South African reds tasted a little
muddy, too, though no doubt the makers would describe it
as 'earthy', which somehow sounds all right. ('Rusticity' is
another good word for the same thing. The wine trade has a
great ability to produce attractive euphemisms.)

Anyhow, the muddiness is now leaving Pinotage. Picking
the grapes when they are really ripe and maturing them in oak
seems to improve the flavour of the wine and make it taste
less as if it has been blended with plant food. Some examples,
like the Pinotage produced by the Warwick Estate and
Beyerskloof, made by Beyers Truter, show the grape variety
at its best: deep, dark, packed with winter fruits. And not a
whiff of damp soil.

However, some people – a minority, to be sure
– liked the muddiness. Anthony Mitchell of El
Vino's once told me that he had a customer who
complained about his Pinotage. 'Haven't you
got anything muddier?' he asked, in the manner
of someone in a grubby raincoat asking for
something stronger in a Soho porn store.

POL ROGER

Champagne, France

SPARKLING ✪✪✪✪—✪✪✪✪✪

A wondrous depth, richness and complexity

In the great Pol Roger cellars at Épernay there is one cellar which holds the superb vintages of the past. When, during the Second World War, the Germans were advancing west across France, the people at Pol Roger bricked the cellar up. Then, realizing that the *Wehrmacht* might be vicious but weren't stupid, they employed someone to 'distress' the brickwork to make it look as if it had been there for hundreds of years. You can imagine the excitement after the war when that wall was taken down.

There are other great champagnes. Certainly there are more plentiful ones (Moët makes around 17 times as much each year.) But Pol Roger has always been especially loved by connoisseurs. It combines great delicacy – some claim to be able to taste hawthorn blossom – with terrific body and power. It was the favourite champagne of Winston Churchill, though this may have had something to do with his *tendresse* for Odette Pol-Roger, daughter-in-law of Maurice, whose genius for public relations made the brand world famous. Their Cuvée Sir Winston Churchill is the absolute top-of-the-line vintage, with a wondrous depth, richness and complexity. But any bottle of Pol Roger, including their basic White Foil, is delicious.

I have a special liking for the people at Pol Roger. Often, when champagne houses serve you a meal, they try to persuade you that you can drink their product with every course. This is not true. You wind up gassy and bloated, as if you had just drunk too many pints of pressurized beer. At Pol Roger they gave us a red Burgundy, a Volnay – from 1926 – to go with the lamb cutlets. It was a great kindness. The Volnay wasn't bad, either.

Pol Roger also employs a reverse public relations firm, whose job it is to keep the marque's name out of the papers, or at least out of the celebrity gossip magazines. The last thing they want is the sight of their bottles being shaken up on Formula One podia, or in shot with rock stars and footballers at a certain type of club.

The Germans were advancing west across France, the people at Pol Roger bricked the cellar up. Then, realizing that the Wehrmacht might be vicious but weren't stupid, they employed someone to 'distress' the brickwork to make it look as if it had been there for hundreds of years. You can imagine the excitement after the war when that wall was taken down.

PROSECCO
Italy
SPARKLING ○○

A light, off-dry sparkler that is increasingly good

Prosecco is what you drink when you go to Venice. By now it is as much a part of the trip as St Mark's Square and the gondoliers. Specifically, if you have the money, you drink Prosecco in Harry's Bar where, with peach pulp, it makes a bellini. It also works well with other fruit juices or syrups: blackcurrant, of course, for a kir royale, or grenadine to make a pomegranate cup, or crushed raspberries. You can also drink it on its own, but it lacks the whoomph and fizz of champagne, and is not especially alcoholic. It is also one of the few sparklers that don't always have a wire cage to keep the cork down; you need to cut the string that helps hold the cork down, then pull it out with a corkscrew. It's not a great wine, but it is a fun wine. It would be perfect for a party in which many guests had to drive home; with its fruity additions it has the ability to make people feel very merry without actually being drunk.

Almost all Prosecco comes from a region about 30 miles north of Venice. For technical buffs, it is a late-ripening grape variety, which means that when cool autumn days arrive it hasn't finished fermenting. This leaves behind carbon dioxide and sugar, creating a light, off-dry sparkler, which is increasingly popular and, thank heavens, increasingly good.

For the most part, makers haven't cashed in by flogging an inferior product. A new denomination (DOCG) came in during April 2010: Conegliano-Valdobbiadene Prosecco Superiore. You can currently get a Conegliano – the Collalbrigo Brut – from FromVineyardsDirect and Vintage Roots do a good one called Bosca del Merlo (both at around a tenner).

PSI
Ribera del Duero, Spain
RED ✪✪✪

Warm, ripe, plump, velvety and packed with flavour

We have heard of Danish pastry, Danish bacon and, recently, Danish TV box sets. Danish wine is new, but like the thrillers and the political dramas on television, they have taken something others already do well and have made it unique.

In this case, the star is the Dane Peter Sisseck, who, more than 20 years ago, went to work near the Ribera del Duero (the same river is known as the Douro in Portugal), which was then a very obscure winemaking area. He had trained in Bordeaux, so knew his business well, and helped establish a reputation for the Hacienda Monasterio. But he wanted to make his own wine, so he selected some small plots he knew would be perfect for creating something that couldn't be found anywhere else in the world. The Tempranillo vines he chose were all at least 60 years old and were growing at heights above 800 metres, which meant warm days but cool nights.

His Pingus wine (not a penguin, but Peter's own nickname) is delectable and extremely expensive. But he set about making other, less pricey wines, paying local growers not for the quantity of the grapes they sold – the old system had meant their main interest was shovelling out as much fruit as possible, by any means available – but for the quality. The result is Psi (a play on his initials as well as being the 23rd letter of the Greek alphabet), and while it is not cheap, it is quite extraordinary value, being warm, ripe, plump, velvety and packed with flavour. But it's more than just a fruit-bomb; it has the elegance that connoisseurs bang on about as well.

PULIGNY-MONTRACHET
Burgundy, France
WHITE ✪✪✪—✪✪✪✪

Just thrilling, with an intense flavour that you never quite forget

Montrachet is the finest white Burgundy of all. Very few people can afford the stuff. Happily we can enjoy a version of it that is a fraction of the price and not all that much less delicious. There is a simple rule-of-thumb. If you buy a £5 bottle of wine, nearly all your money is going on tax, duty, bottling, carriage costs and in some cases, publicity. Only coppers are paying for the actual fluid. Apart from VAT, those costs are scarcely any higher in a medium-priced wine, which means that a much higher proportion of your money is going on the wine itself. So you're getting better value. And if you buy a really expensive wine, such as Montrachet, you are paying for the name. If you're not very rich, it's not worth bothering.

Puligny is a pleasant village to the east of the area and, as is common in Burgundy, is allowed to attach the most famous local vineyard to its name. It was a *négociant* from this neck of the woods my wife and I met at the celebrated Hospices de Beaune during a tasting, and we were staying, it emerged, near his home. Why, he said, when we were next there, we should come and try some of his wines, along with local foods. 'And,' he added, gazing at my wife, 'if your 'usband cannot come, you would be moze welcome on your own…' I mentioned this to a young woman in the wine trade in London. 'Yes, I know who that was,' she said. 'We've never met, but he does exactly the same thing to me – down the phone.'

A good Puligny-Montrachet is just thrilling, with an intense flavour you never quite forget. And for £25+ you'll still get a very good one.

ANDREW QUADY
ELYSIUM BLACK MUSCAT

Central Valley, California, USA

FORTIFIED ✪✪—✪✪✪

Even locals admit that California's Central Valley isn't much to look at. With neither the manicured elegance of the Napa Valley nor the raw beauty of Mendocino County, it's an unprepossessing place. Drearily flat, its scattered orchards, vineyards and fields of scrub are divided by straight roads boasting such inspiring names as Avenue 12 and Road 24.

But here at California's heart, just outside Madera, north-west of Fresno, the madly eccentric Andrew Quady makes one of my favourite sweet wines: Elysium Black Muscat.

Rose petal aromas, glorious grapey sweetness and fine acidity

I'm a sucker for sweet wines. They're wonderfully versatile and we do them a disservice by pigeon-holing them as so-called dessert wines. They're far more flexible than that and go with rich foie gras or smoked fish starters and all manner of cheeses just as well as they do with pudding.

Strangely, though, one thing most sweet wines don't go with is chocolate. Try a Sauternes, say, alongside a chocolate mousse and you ruin both. The exception is Elysium.

Andrew Quady got bitten by the wine bug whilst working in an explosives factory in the 1970s. He quit his job after the bunker exploded one Christmas Eve and enrolled in a winemaking course at UC Davis.

He began by making port-style wines from Zinfandel and then, having tasted some Muscat de Beaumes de Venise in France, made a lightly fortified sweet wine from Orange Muscat which he called Essensia. It was a thundering success.

In 1983 he discovered Black Muscat, a grape which supposedly originated in England in the 1700s, and whose parent is probably the famous Black Hamburg vine at Hampton Court. A grower who made sacramental wine for a local church was stuck with truckloads of ripe Black Muscat when the church went bust and Andrew grabbed the lot and never looked back.

Among the great Quady's other wine treats, none are equal to Elysium with its rose petal aromas, glorious grapey sweetness and fine acidity. Enjoy it with chocolate, with cheese or poured over vanilla ice cream. Best of all, enjoy it on its own.

DOMAINE
RICHEAUME

APPELLATION CÔTES DE PROVENCE CONTRÔLÉE
CUVÉE TRADITION

Deep, rich and
very delicious

DOMAINE RICHEAUME
CUVÉE TRADITION
CÔTES DE PROVENCE
Provence, France
RED ○○

Southwold is a fine seaside town on the Suffolk coast. It is
remorselessly middle-class, even wealthy. Last time I looked,
beach huts cost around £40,000 each. There are parts of
England where that would almost buy you an entire house.
But it has a smashing beach, an exciting pier, two fine
hotels, the Swan and the Crown (the latter having a superb
restaurant) and a string of first-rate pubs, all but one of
which belong to Adnams, the local brewer. At times the
smell of brewing permeates the town. I quite like it – a
comforting, toasty aroma – but, if you don't, at least you
can reflect that it is a by-product of creating some of the
best beers in the country.

Adnams also ships wine, and has some very intriguing
bottles on show in its wine and kitchen shop. It's well worth
a visit, since the company always has interesting offers.
For instance, it does a sort of vinous pick 'n' mix, with any
combination of a dozen bottles from one set of shelves for,
say, £59.99, or grander choices for £79.99. There are also
weekend tastings, which some locals regard as an extension
of their social life. I recall a very *grande dame* sitting near the
sample table and asking for more white Burgundy. 'Fill the
glass, please!' she said crisply. This was not a tasting portion.

I spoke at a wine lunch in the Crown one year, and with
the main course we were offered Domaine Richeaume Cuvée
Tradition. This is a Provençal wine, made by a biodynamic
German *vigneron*, Henning Hoesch, a history professor who
also plays the cello. In 1972 he started with just two hectares
of vines. Now he has 25, and uses them to make several
different wines, of which this is my favourite. It is roughly
half Cabernet Sauvignon and half Syrah, and it is deep, rich
and very delicious.

I recall a very grande dame sitting hard by
the sample table and asking for more white
Burgundy. 'Fill the glass, please!' she said
crisply. This was not a tasting portion.

It will improve in bottle for a good five years. Perhaps
the flavour is due in part to the flock of sheep Hoesch keeps
to provide organic fertilizer, though it would be a very bold
wine writer who claimed to detect 'top notes
of sheep droppings'.

In any event, when I popped into the Adnams shop to
acquire some Richeaume for myself, it had completely sold
out to the happy lunchers.

RIDGE CALIFORNIA MONTE BELLO

Santa Cruz Mountains, California

RED ○○○○○

Packed with myriad perfumes and undertones, and the warm, cedary, leathery flavours a great Cabernet Sauvignon offers

This is a superlative wine, packed with myriad perfumes and undertones, and the warm, cedary, leathery flavours that a great Cabernet Sauvignon offers. In the past, many California winemakers felt their wines lacked 'backbone, that degree of power, almost austerity, possessed by the finest Bordeaux reds'. This is no longer the case. Monte Bello is the epitome of what a great wine should be, and if you ever manage to get the opportunity to try it, do so.

The winery isn't in the Napa Valley, but south of San Francisco Bay, high above the fog line, very close to San José. Ridge wines had fallen into desuetude, but were revived 30 years ago by Paul Draper. He was not an oenologist, but had studied philosophy at Stanford. Then he turned his hand to winemaking and set up a vineyard in Chile, returning to take over at Ridge. Under his guidance, the old winery, which had been run in much the same way for decades by the Perrone family, was restored. The finest vineyards in the region were bought or leased, and it wasn't long before Ridge wines had won an international reputation.

Draper and his team are more interested in helping nature gently and using traditional methods rather than the latest fashionable technology. The result is a series of wines with intense, rich, direct flavours that justifiably command whopping prices. Actually, their great speciality has been Zinfandel, the California grape that is not usually held in great esteem by Europeans. Much of it goes to make an unpleasing 'blush' wine, which is a watery-looking rosé (best avoided). The Ridge Zinfandels are a different matter.

However, it is really Monte Bello Cabernet that has made the winery famous around the world. Draper uses old vines, ages in American oak and produces a wine more like a Bordeaux than some Bordeaux. Which must make his triumph in the Judgement of Paris (see pages 84–86) no less upsetting to the Bordelais.

RUSTENBERG
JOHN X MERRIMAN
Stellenbosch, South Africa
RED ✪✪

It has the weight
and plumpness of a
really good claret

South African wine seems very new to many modern
drinkers. In the days of apartheid, few people bought
it, and few merchants wanted to court trouble by selling
it, even if they were indifferent to interests of the black
majority population. Or, 'I'm not interested in politics,' as
people tended to put it, as if politics were something you
could separate from your life, as in 'I'm not interested in
trainspotting. Or bondage wear.' I am reminded of the story
told by the late Paul Foot, the campaigning journalist. He
was buying oranges at a greengrocer. 'Just a minute,' he
said. 'These are from South Africa. I'm not buying them.'
'Quite right,' said the shopkeeper, 'all those black hands
picking them.'

But the Rustenberg estate goes back to 1682, when a farmer
from Meurs, near the Rhine, spotted its potential for wine-
growing. Over the years – including the Great Trek, the Boer
War, the establishment of apartheid, the Sharpeville Massacre
and the release of Nelson Mandela – it passed through several
owners, including John X Merriman, who bought half the
estate in 1892 and who later became prime minister of the
Cape. Peter and Pamela Barlow bought it in 1941, and in 1987
their son Simon took over and set about bringing the vineyards
up to date.

Rustenberg is now regarded as one of the finest estates in
South Africa, making a fine range of wines from Bordeaux
blends to Syrah, Chardonnay and Sauvignon Blanc. They make
a delicious, if hard-to-pronounce white called Schoongezicht,
which is a blend of southern French grapes, including Sémillon,
Viognier and Roussanne. Rich, fat and full, you may need to
pluck it from the shelf rather than try to ask the merchant if
he has it in stock. I really like the their Bordeaux-style John X
Merriman, named in honour of the earlier owner. It has the
weight and plumpness of a really good claret – at a very, very
good price. Another bottle to turn a fine meal into a feast.

SAINT-AUBIN
Burgundy, France
RED & WHITE ✪✪–✪✪✪

All the heady perfume of the finest Burgundies, but with an added depth that tastes of vanilla and hazelnuts

You should always distinguish between wine snobs and wine experts. Wine snobs place great importance on names. They resemble social snobs, to whom titles also matter greatly. If they are looking at Burgundy, for example, they will see names such as Montrachet, or La Tâche, and nod approvingly. Of course these wines are very fine indeed, often magnificent, but they have price tags attached which reflect all this grandeur – and more.

By contrast, your wine expert knows that it's the contents of the bottle that count. He or she, refusing to be bamboozled by famous names, ferrets out good stuff from lesser-known areas: wines that have no great public relations, which rarely figure on the menus of state banquets, and aren't glugged back by Russian billionaires. These wines are often the best value.

Take Chorey-lès-Beaune, a tiny appellation near the town of Beaune. Much of the wine is sold as generic Beaune Burgundy, but some of it is superb, and costs a fraction of what you would pay for the greater names. You might try Tollot-Beaut, and be very agreeably surprised.

Saint-Aubin is, perhaps, its white equivalent. A good one has all the heady perfume of the finest Burgundies, but has an added depth that tastes of vanilla and hazelnuts. People who try this wine often adore it – and you can generally get a good one for around £15 a bottle. Olivier Leflaive is a reliable provider.

You should always distinguish between wine
snobs and wine experts. Wine snobs place
great importance on names. They resemble
social snobs, to whom titles also matter greatly.
If they are looking at Burgundy, for example,
they will see names such as Montrachet, or La
Tache, and nod approvingly.

SAINT-CHINIAN
Languedoc-Roussillon, France
RED ○○

It ought to be more famous than it is

If you really want good-value French wines, the place to look is the south. I recall a magnum of Saint-Chinian one Christmas Eve. We had made a pheasant casserole, plumped up with shallots, mushrooms and red wine, served with green beans and a small mountain of earthy fir apple potatoes. The wine was smooth, silky, spicy, herby, a hint of earth matching the potatoes, the whole with a tangy note of sour cherries. It made a feast that would match any Christmas Day dinner.

Saint-Chinian is a small, rocky *appellation* in the very south of France. The rules are complicated; you can have only 40 per cent of the Carignan grape variety, but in Saint-Chinian Berlou (as opposed to the other part of the area, Saint-Chinian Roquebrun) you must include at least 30 per cent Carignan, but no more than 30 per cent Cinsault.

By this time any grower's head would be spinning, so no doubt he throws in a handful each of the other permitted varieties, including Syrah, Grenache, Mourvèdre, and a grape of which few people have heard, the Lladoner Pelut, which the Spanish call 'hairy Grenache' as the leaves have more fur on their underside than most vines.

You do not need to know any of this to enjoy the taste of Saint-Chinian. My favourite is Canet-Valette, which ought to be more famous than it is.

SANTA RITA RESERVAS, TRIPLE C & LOS VASCOS

Maipo Valley, Chile

RED ○○

Santa Rita is Chile's most successful winery. I like them as they gave me a decanter that improves red wine faster than any I know. Its low, very bulbous bottom, as if a regular decanter had gone pear-shaped then kept on drooping, is filled to its widest part by a bottle of wine, thus giving it maximum exposure to air. Perfect when friends drop in unexpectedly.

It doesn't have to be Santa Rita, though that would do very nicely. The firm has estates all over the country, but is centred on Buin in the Maipo Valley, about halfway up the country. This is, roughly, the Chilean equivalent of Valley Forge. In 1814, Bernardo O'Higgins, the national liberator, holed up in an underground wine cellar with 120 men during the Battle of Rancagua. This was the decisive engagement against the Spanish, and four years later Chile won its independence. The biggest-selling Santa Rita brand is called '120' in their honour.

There is a wide range of wines, but I like the *reservas* best, including their Chardonnay, Sauvignon Blanc, Merlot and Cabernet. There is also a rather delicious blend called 'Triple C', which is made from Cabernet Sauvignon, Cabernet Franc and Carmenère grapes.

Santa Rita has a share in another Bordeaux-style Chilean wine, Los Vascos, made by a team from Château Lafite-Rothschild, one of the celebrated (and expensive) first growth clarets. Some experts are snippy about Los Vascos, but I like it a lot – especially as you can get two or three cases for the price of a bottle of most first-growth clarets. It comes on nicely if you leave it for an hour or two in a Santa Rita decanter.

All the aromas of herbs with a peachy, nutty background

DOMAINE SAPARALE
CORSE SARTÈNE BLANC

Corsica, France

WHITE ●●

Napoleon came from Corsica, and in exile on Elba he claimed he could smell the thyme and lavender of the Corsican *maquis*, or scrub, wafted on the breeze, reminding him of the home he would never see again. Mind you, Corsica is about as different from the genteel vineyards of, say, Bordeaux and Burgundy, as you can imagine. Even quite ordinary houses there can be fortified against the blood feuds that marked the island's long, fraught history.

When they can spare time from vendettas, they do make delicious wine. Corsicans are loathe to part with it – like most French regions they are fiercely proud of their local wine and regard most others as inferior rot-gut. Indeed much of their local stuff is of very high quality, so it's not always easy to find this one. It's made on an estate that was founded in the late 19th century, when it was vast, employing more than a hundred people. Then wars and phylloxera struck, and it dwindled into decay, in the end producing table fruit but no wine.

Now it has been revived, and in the last decade, worked by Philippe Farinelli, has started to produce this marvellous white wine from the Vermentino grape. It blends all the aromas of herbs with a peachy, nutty background. The slight metallic undertone is like some Chablis; if you were fanciful you might imagine that a few stray bullets found their way into the casks. It is perfect with seafood, and a very reasonable price, so you can offer loads to your friends.

VILLA BIZZARRI SASSO ARSO MONTEPULCIANO D'ABRUZZO

Abruzzo, Italy

RED ✪✪

This wine is here partly because every element of it cheers me. *Sasso arso* means 'burnt stone', indicating the extreme local temperatures. Montepulciano is the grape variety, which doesn't make the greatest Italian wines, but handled with care, as at the Villa Bizzarri, it has lovely cherry and liquorice flavours, and doesn't cost much. It is quite remarkable value, and friends will roar with laughter at the label. Sadly, it is nearly impossible to find in the UK at the moment, but if you look hard enough, you can try other wines from the same stable. For example, Corney & Barrow currently imports Villa Bizzarri's Montepulciano d'Abruzzo Roccastella.

Lovely cherry and liquorice flavours

IS IT WORTH IT?

The question I am most often asked, especially about expensive wines, is 'Can it be worth that?' The answer, when it comes to wines costing thousands of pounds a bottle, is almost certainly not. At least not for us.

If you are so wealthy you can afford £3,600 for a bottle of Le Pin as easily as the rest of us stump up for a newspaper, then it is worth it. You'd probably enjoy it very much, not least because you have the intense pleasure and satisfaction of knowing you can afford it.

If, by contrast, you or I were bonkers enough to sell a car in order to buy the same bottle, it's likely we'd be crushingly disappointed. 'It's very nice,' you might think, 'very nice indeed. But not that incredibly nice: not as nice as a holiday for two in Barbados. And I haven't got a car any more…'

You can pay £7,000 for a bottle of La Romanée-Conti. Is it 140 times as good as a £50 Burgundy? Or 700 times as good as a generic red Burgundy at a tenner? Would you rather have the one bottle or the £700? It's not a tricky question.

If you have enough savvy and confidence to acquire some classic wines, you can drink great vintages for nothing. Adam Brett-Smith of Corney & Barrow says that you can buy, say, a case of Domaine de la Romanée-Conti, the most celebrated of all red Burgundies, when it first comes on the market for several thousand pounds. It will at least double in value as it ages, so in, say, seven years you can sell half the case for what you paid for the dozen and drink the rest yourself. That would be worth it: if you have so much money to tie up and are prepared to take the risk.

Of course the principle works at the other end of the scale, too. Just as a book costing £1.99 is no bargain if you don't read it, and £18.99 is a good price for the new novel by your favourite author, so a really cheap wine can be as much of a rip-off as something much more expensive. My heart always sinks when someone tells me what a minuscule price they paid for something they bought at a supermarket in Calais. It's probably priced so low because that's what it's worth – and in any event the makers have no hope of exporting it.

It's all a matter of taste and circumstance. In this book I mention a bottle of Latour's Bâtard-Montrachet. It was so inexpressibly delicious, so head- and mind-fillingly gorgeous, that I rang my daughter to say I had found the wine for her wedding; at least we might run to two bottles for the bride, the groom and the parents. This in spite of the fact that she was in Sri Lanka at the time, and had absolutely no plans to get married. Each bottle would have cost £160 or more, yet for something that stays in the memory forever (a daughter's wedding), it would be very well worth it. To give it to friends who popped round for a fish supper would be dementedly spendthrift.

So whether a wine is 'worth it' depends on many different factors and occasions. You've just picked up a take-away curry. A bottle of a nice, meaty Côtes du Rhône at £6 would wash that down very nicely, but then so might a spicy but dry Italian white: say, a Pinot Grigio for £7 or so. Old friends come round for dinner, and a couple of £10 bottles of Domaine Richeaume are just the ticket; after all, few restaurants would sell you any wine for that price, and they'd probably charge around £35 for the Richeaume. So you've got a bargain there. A bottle of Pétalos del Bierzo from northern Spain would be delicious with the Christmas turkey, whereas the cheaper Vernaccia di San Gimignano

helps lift the Boxing Day leftovers. Your son gets the two As and a B he needs to get to university, so a bottle of the Camel Valley Pinot Noir sparkling seems a snip at £29.95.

I don't think it's entirely fanciful to say that you can taste whether a wine has been made to make money or because the maker loves to make wine.

I happen not to like most of the big, mass-produced branded wines – not out of snobbery or some notion that only the riff-raff drink them, but because they taste mass-produced. I don't think it's entirely fanciful to say that you can taste whether a wine has been made to make money or because the maker loves to make wine. To me, a bottle of Blossom Hill wouldn't be 'worth it', simply because I wouldn't enjoy drinking it. I'd rather have a cold beer. Others might, which is why you could possibly win it on the tombola stall at our local fair – which is where I have taken the bottle someone brought round, meaning to be kind.

SAVENNIÈRES
Loire Valley, France
WHITE ○○

Luscious wines, reminiscent of spring flowers, minerals, dried fruit, limes

Most white wines don't age all that well. Even a good one can be a touch disappointing after a year, distinctly off-colour after two, and undrinkable after three. Many demand to be drunk more or less as soon as you get them home. (Few of us have cellars, or could be bothered to stock them if we had.) The best white Burgundies do age well, but they are the exception. Even a really expensive wine like a fine Condrieu has to be knocked back fairly quickly.

One exception is Chenin Blanc, a grape that used to be roughly as fashionable as flared trousers are today. Often it makes a thin, weedy, flabby wine – the kind I tend to associate with in-flight meals. If you're sitting in the back of the plane, it makes a good way of washing down that lasagne made from recycled in-flight magazines.

Made with love, care and sympathy, though, Chenin can create superb wines. In the Loire Valley there are several appellations which produce the goods, thanks to huge care and attention, and the plucking of selected individual bunches of grapes – even in some mad cases, single grapes. My own favourite is Savennières, which is made on the very edge of the Anjou area. In particular there is a minute sub-appellation called La Coulée-de-Serrant, fewer than a dozen acres, on a rock spur overlooking the Loire. These are luscious wines, reminiscent of spring flowers, minerals, dried fruit, limes, and lots of other things besides. And they can be laid down for years.

Often it makes a thin, weedy, flabby wine – the kind I tend to associate with in-flight meals. If you're sitting in the back of the plane, it makes a good way of washing down that lasagne made from recycled in-flight magazines.

Soft, supple, succulent, spicy

SERESIN ESTATE 'LEAH' PINOT NOIR

Marlborough, New Zealand

RED ✪✪✪

There's already a very fine trio of New Zealand wines listed in these pages but so good have Kiwi wines become that I just have to mention a fourth: Seresin Estate 'Leah' Pinot Noir.

Situated in the heart of Marlborough, Seresin Estate is owned by Michael Seresin, the wine-besotted cinematographer who made his name photographing such movies as *Angela's Ashes*, *Midnight Express*, *Fame*, *Harry Potter and the Prisoner of Azkaban* and *Dawn of the Planet of the Apes*.

Unsurprisingly, given his day job, Michael has an extraordinary eye for detail and by all accounts drives his team mad, not only when he's away filming or at his homes in London and Tuscany but also when he's in New Zealand not filming. He's either impossible to get hold of (he hates email) or impossible to get rid of (he gets in the way, obsessively checking up on this and that).

But thanks to Michael's single-mindedness and deep pockets, Seresin Estate has built itself a formidable reputation with its finely textured Sauvignon Blancs and Chardonnays and big, silky Pinot Noirs, produced in the most natural method possible. Only fruit grown on the estate's own organic and biodynamic vineyards is used – something of a rarity in Marlborough – and all grapes are hand-picked.

I adore the wines of New Zealand and would happily drink nothing but. There are the exceptional Pinot Noirs of Central Otago, Martinborough and Marlborough; the remarkable Bordeaux blends and Syrahs of the Gimblett Gravels, Hawkes Bay; the aromatic whites of Nelson and Gisborne and fine sparklers such as Pelorus from Cloudy Bay as well as sumptuously delicious sweet wines. Top of the pile, though, is Seresin Estate, home to wines with – as Michael puts it – both mystery and complexity. The half dozen or so different Pinot Noirs made here are stunning. The top of the range 'Sun & Moon' Pinot Noir (around £60 a pop) is a cracker, but my favourite is the entry-level 'Leah', named after Michael's daughter and blended from the estate's three different vineyards. It's soft, supple, succulent, spicy and vibrantly fresh with bright berry fruit and a touch of herbs – and I just love it.

SHERRY

Jerez, Spain

FORTIFIED ✪—✪✪

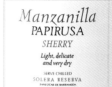

Dry enough to make your palate tingle

What wine is the best value in the world? Many experts and amateur drinkers would say sherry. You can get a bottle of a truly first-rate sherry for the same price as a tolerable but unexceptional bottle of many common-or-garden table wines. Sherries can be subtle and varied. They range from bone-dry to warm, rich and sweet. What's not to like? The image, mainly.

The best news sherry ever had – its name is from the southwestern Spanish region of Jerez, where all the real stuff is made – came in 1587, when Sir Francis Drake attacked Cádiz harbour and made off with 3,000 casks, which he took back to London. The capital was soon sluicing with sherry, which became immediately fashionable, and which didn't lose ground for centuries. It was a respectable drink. Aunts or vicars, or university dons, who would no more keep beer or gin in the house than they would offer their guests a spliff, were happy to sip at a sherry. It became a by-word for gentility. John Mortimer has a story about an elderly magistrate binding over a drunken vagrant not to touch alcohol: 'not even the teeniest dry sherry before luncheon'.

There were the roots of its decline. In 1979, they exported one-and-a-half billion litres of sherry, much of which was just not up to standard. Ten years later it was half that quantity. To modern drinkers all round the world, sherry was a bit of a joke, something your nan kept in a dusty bottle to be brought out at Christmas.

Now there is a bit of a comeback, as a fresh generation of drinkers discover the many pleasures of sherry. There are innumerable different styles all made in a different fashion, but basically the light, dry Sherries such as fino are created by *flor*, a natural yeast that lies on top of the wine and the fortifying grape spirit. My own favourite is manzanilla, which is dry enough to make your palate tingle and is thought to have a salty tang from the sea. An oloroso is thicker and darker, though not necessarily sweeter, and has been fortified to the point where the *flor* is killed off. You really don't need to know an awful lot more, except that some sweet versions, often made from the Pedro Ximénez grape (known as PX, and very popular in Spain itself) are unimaginably different from anything your Aunt Edna might have hoarded under the title of Cream Sherry.

An extraordinary
wine you either
love or loathe

SILEX CHARDONNAY, LE MAS DES MASQUES
Provence, France
WHITE ✪✪

This is an extraordinary wine. Sometimes people compare it to Marmite, on the grounds that you either love it or loathe it. Actually the real division is between people who, on the one hand, absolutely adore it, and on the other, those who can take it or leave it.

It is made at Le Mas des Masques in Provence (*Mas* is the dialect word for 'farm' and *Silex* is the name of the dominant stone in the land) and it is all Chardonnay. But what Chardonnay! People who tell you they are bored with Chardonnay and would like any other grape clearly have not tried this. For one thing it is blended from two vintages – the bottles I tasted combine 2007 and 2008 – and that's unusual enough. Then it is oxidized ever so slightly, which gives it a more mature and rounded taste, though some people think it reminds them a shade unpleasantly of wine that is on the turn.

It's imported here by Swig, a firm in west London, which has collected comments from its customers. Many of them think it tastes like one of the finest white Burgundies, sold at a fraction of the cost. They compare it to Puligny-Montrachet, or even Meursault. They place orders for future vintages. Others find it overoaked and fat – the whole effect too overwhelming.

It is most certainly a wine that grabs your attention from the moment you first sniff it. You really should try it if you can.

SOLI PINOT NOIR
Thrace, Bulgaria
RED ✪✪

Smoothness, perfume, body and ripeness

This is the kind of wine that makes fools of the experts. Bung the word 'Bulgarian' on any label and you turn most wine-lovers into wary hedgehogs, stiff and prickling with suspicion. In fact, Bulgarian wine is one of those we drank when we were students, because it was full and meaty, and best of all, cheap. Many people would pass it by at the supermarket in the 'two for £3.99' bin.

This is very different. The team at Swig, whose staff go out of their way to discover new treasures, offers it in blind tastings to customers who almost invariably rave about its smoothness, perfume, body, ripeness, flavours of sour cherries and forest fruits and all that good stuff. It is made by Edoardo Miroglio, an Italian textile magnate who wanted to make a wine that would rival red Burgundy but couldn't think of buying the incredibly expensive land in Burgundy itself.

So he set about finding the right soil and the right climate somewhere less pricey. Miroglio discovered his patch of land in what used to be called Thrace, and is now part of Bulgaria. He sank 22 million euros into the project, and, thanks to his own dedication (and, of course, modern technology), he produced this wine that fools almost everyone who drinks it into thinking it really is Burgundy – at half or one-third the price.

Soli is delicious when you buy it, but will go on improving for three or four years. Frankly, I would decant it, so that your friends can 'ooh' and 'ah' before they learn where it comes from.

CHÂTEAU DE SOURS

Bordeaux, France

ROSÉ ⊙⊙

It can claim much of the credit for restoring the good name of pink wines

For years rosé wines were the object of much derision. 'Real' wine drinkers didn't think of them as wines at all – more like alcoholic sherbet dabs. They were the wines for people who didn't actually like wine very much. If you drank rosé at all, it was in high summer when there was nothing really worth drinking around. I also suspect that pink wines suffered from the popularity of the giant brands, such as Mateus from Portugal. The older generation felt they had outgrown the stuff, while younger folk thought it hopelessly old-fashioned.

Recently that has changed completely. Wine merchants report huge increases in the sales of rosés. A while ago I sat near a couple eating in the extremely posh Café des Anglais in Bayswater. They polished off a bottle of rosé with their spit-roast chicken. Not surprising, perhaps, except that outside it was an extremely cold January day.

One of the main reasons for this shift in attitudes is simply that rosés are now much better. They tend to have real oomph and flavour. This Château de Sours can claim much of the credit for restoring the good name of pink wines. It is a Bordeaux château, and what it has made is essentially a see-through version of claret. Indeed, the English word 'claret' (not used in France) originally referred to the fact that red Bordeaux wines were *claire* – that is, translucent. This wine has all the refreshing qualities of a good white wine, but bags of the flavour we associate with the Bordeaux grape varieties: Cabernet Sauvignon, Merlot and so forth.

You can make a fake rosé by adding a little red wine to colour a white wine, but that's cheating and, in any case, doesn't taste the same. Most rosé wines these days are made by short-term maceration, which merely means that the skins of red grapes are left in with the juice for a few hours. The tinted and flavoured liquor is then poured off and left to ferment in the usual way. The result is, basically, a wine with the qualities of both reds and whites. No wonder rosé is so popular these days.

SPY VALLEY SAUVIGNON BLANC & PINOT NOIR

Marlborough, New Zealand

WHITE & RED ✪

Marlborough, at the northern tip of the South Island, is one of the newest wine regions in New Zealand. Almost no wine was produced here until 1973, and now there are more than 100 growers, producing some of the country's very best wines: Sauvignon Blanc, Pinot Noir, Riesling, Gewurztraminer. Their Sauvignon Blancs set the template for that grape variety all round the world, forcing the French in the Loire to raise their game considerably and find new ways of bringing flavour to the flintiness.

Delectable and life-improving – it seems almost to leap out of the glass at you

Did you know that, of all wine-producing countries, New Zealand fetches the highest average price? This is because they make no plonk at all. It's all good stuff. The most famous name in Marlborough is Cloudy Bay, which used to be superb, but has, in most people's view, gone downhill. Of course when you establish a brand, you can go on charging what you always did, which is why it's often priced at £50 or £60 in restaurants. Don't pay it. Some of the growers who used to sell their grapes to Cloudy Bay now produce their own wine, which is usually much better value.

One example is Spy Valley, which is the local name for the Waihopai Valley. The nickname comes from the fact that the Americans established a listening post here. I think their Sauvignon Blanc is delectable and life-improving – it seems almost to leap out of the glass at you. After you have had the first sip you feel much more cheerful, because you know there is the rest of the bottle to come. But their Pinot Noir is plump and gorgeous, too. Spy Valley wines seem to get better every year; if you see them in your local shop, you should really try them.

TALTARNI TACHÉ
Victoria, Australia
SPARKLING ✪✪

It is impossible to separate wines from the circumstances in which you drink them: a celebration, perhaps, a cosy dinner with friends, or in the case of this gorgeous sparkler, a picnic in Northamptonshire. Not many people who don't live there realize that this is one of the most beautiful counties in England. Gentle rolling hills and honey-coloured stone buildings make it a secret version of the Cotswolds. Here one April, beside a gurgling stream, wild flowers dotted on the grass, the sun bringing just enough warmth to keep us comfortable, we opened up paper packets of pâté and cheese, and filled our plastic glasses with this delicious pink wine.

Strictly speaking, it's a cheat. The basic wine is made in the same way as champagne and with the same grape varieties – Chardonnay and Pinot Noir. Plus some Pinot Meunier. *Meunier* means 'miller', and rather pleasingly refers to the fact that the vine leaves have a dusty white underside. It's also a good variety to grow in somewhat cooler climes, such as Tasmania. It ripens early and adds a nice fruity plumpness. Then the Taltarni people colour it ('*taché*' means 'stained') by adding just a bit of red-wine liqueur, which gives it a nice deep-salmon colour without, to be frank, adding anything you'd notice to the flavour. It's a really cheerful wine, a terrific pick-me-up, a perfect first drink of the day. And it costs far less than pink champagne.

TAPANAPPA FOGGY HILL PINOT NOIR

South Australia

RED ✪✪✪—✪✪✪✪

We in the UK drink more wine from Australia than we do from anywhere else. Sadly, most of what we knock back is bland, unexciting, mass-produced generic junk bought for a song in the supermarket. We should be more adventurous, for there is so much more to Australia than simply the likes of Banrock Station, Hardy's and Jacob's Creek.

Brian Croser has crafted a deliciously juicy and mellow wine

There are, after all, 65 different official wine regions in Australia, in many cases thousands of miles apart, all boasting utterly different terroirs, grapes, blends and styles.

Simon has picked seven extremely toothsome examples to demonstrate what is so exciting and diverse about Australian wine today but I would be failing in my duty if I didn't draw your attention to an eighth, the exquisite Tapanappa Foggy Hill Pinot Noir from Fleurieu Peninsula in South Australia.

Tapanappa was founded jointly in 2002 by three titans of the wine world: Brian Croser (founder of Petaluma), Jean-Michel Cazes (owner of Château Lynch-Bages) and the Bollinger family of champagne fame.

Today, Tapanappa is wholly owned by the Croser family and they concentrate on producing cool-climate wines that speak of their unique terroir: a Chardonnay, a Cabernet Sauvignon and a Pinot Noir. Fabulous though all their wines are, for my money the Pinot is the ace in the pack.

Pinot is a sod of a grape to grow, being thin-skinned and susceptible to mildew, rot and frost and very picky about its soil. The good folk of Burgundy would have you believe that theirs is the only place in the world in which Pinot is happy. Others would disagree, pointing out that although Pinot Noir is bloody-minded and capricious (not for nothing is it known as the heartbreak grape), it also thrives in tiny, far-flung sweet spots in such diverse places as Alsace, South Africa, New Zealand, California and Oregon.

Here, just south of Adelaide, is another super-sweet spot and Brian Croser has crafted a deliciously juicy and mellow wine with smoky dark berry fruit and a gloriously soft, ever so slightly spicy finish. Only 1,800 dozen bottles were made of the current (2013) vintage. Grab some if you can.

PARKER COONAWARRA ESTATE TERRA ROSSA CABERNET SAUVIGNON

Coonawarra, South Australia

RED ✪✪✪

Delicious, with style, richness and finesse

It seems inconceivable now, but less than 40 years ago, Monty Python was still making jokes about Australian wine. They were remembering what was sometimes called 'Empire wine' – usually thick, sweet, alcoholic goo. 'This is not a wine for drinking now. It is a wine for laying down and forgetting about,' was one of the lines. It was already unfair.

Now only the French would disagree that Australia is one of the very greatest wine-producing nations. Not everybody loves those great starburst flavours, but we can all agree that they do have superb qualities and reflect the highest standards of winemaking. And increasingly, just as the French are trying to pump more flavour into their wines in order to hold on to international sales, the Australians are experimenting to bring a sense of place, of what the French call *terroir*, to their wines.

And few places are more distinctive than the Terra Rossa of South Australia. This is a patch of red soil perhaps nine miles long by one mile wide, four or five hours' drive south of Adelaide in the Coonawarra region.

Few people live here, and the local town Penola is scarcely a village. But the land is extraordinary. The rich red soil is just 18 inches deep. Underneath is limestone, which drains easily, and six feet under that is a water table that seems never to be dry. In other words, it is perfect for the growing of vines, and particularly for making Bordeaux-style wines. Parker's Terra Rossa Cabernet Sauvignon is delicious, with style, richness and finesse. It costs a fraction of the price you would pay for a Bordeaux of remotely similar quality.

TIGNANELLO
Tuscany, Italy
RED ✪✪✪✪

Among the first of Italy's Super-Tuscan wines

People sometimes ask if they 'should' like a particular wine, which is an absurd question, implying that there is some moral imperative in play here. I don't think I 'should' like broccoli, or Cliff Richard's Christmas records, or *London Fields* by Martin Amis – though, to be fair, I think that novel deserves more consideration than, say, the latest Mills & Boon. At a Christmas wine tasting, the secretary/PA of a very rich and powerful man came to me and asked, 'What wine would Duncan like?', as if there were something that appealed in particular to men of wealth and position. Whether you are a duke or a dustman, a complete amateur in the field or a Master of Wine, it really is a matter of personal taste.

But that doesn't make it entirely haphazard. The great majority of people will prefer, say, a good white Burgundy to a bottle of Blossom Hill Chardonnay, or a fine Australian Shiraz compared to the same thing made by Jacob's Creek. The pricier wines are richer, more complex, more rewarding. They taste nicer. If you prefer the cheapo versions, you're lucky.

In the same way, we grow into better wines. As a student I drank a lot of cheap stuff: German Liebfraumilch, the odd branded French wine (generally to be avoided), something called Bull's Blood from Hungary, which enjoyed a vogue at the time. But then my friends and I discovered that for a few shillings more we could afford wines like the Antinoris from northern Italy, and I have kept my affection for them ever since, even though they have now become one of the biggest wine producers in the country.

Members of the Antinori family have been making wine for more than 800 years, but it wasn't until 1900 that they bought vineyards in the famous Chianti Classico region. They set about an ambitious programme of modernization and experimentation. They used Bordeaux grapes and scandalized the Chianti authorities. In 1971, they introduced a wine called Tignanello, which contained Cabernet Sauvignon and Cabernet Franc. It still does, though 85 per cent of the grapes are local Sangiovese. It wasn't the first 'Super Tuscan' wine, but it may be the most famous, and it costs an awful lot more than I used to pay when I was a student. But it is worth it.

TOKAJI
Hungary
SWEET WHITE ✪✪✪—✪✪✪✪✪

The Gay Hussar is certainly the best-known Hungarian
restaurant in London, and a great deal better than most
restaurants in Hungary. The ground floor is designed like
a luxurious bus, with plush velour benches. The best-known
customers – politicians (chiefly, though not exclusively,
of the Left), journalists, proper writers and trade-union
leaders – are memorialized in cartoons which line the walls.
Many are almost forgotten now; other faces will be puzzling
lunchers in the years to come. For 34 years, the proprietor
and maître d' was Victor Sassie, who was one of Soho's great
characters, and like most characters, was best savoured in
small doses. He saw it as his business to control every aspect
of the restaurant's operation, not least what the customers
chose to eat. I once eavesdropped this conversation:

Victor: 'What have you ordered?'
Customer: 'Roast pork.'
Victor: 'Nah, you don't want that. You want the goose.'
Customer: 'But I don't like goose.'
Victor: 'Nah, there's too much garlic in the pork. The
  girls in the office won't want to kiss you.'
Customer: 'But I don't want the girls in the office to
  kiss me.'
Victor (to the waiter): 'Bring this customer the goose.'

Victor also once threw out the then Foreign Secretary
George Brown for groping a female customer at the
next table.

Portions were, and are, huge. The roast goose is excellent.
So are the goulash and the stuffed cabbage. Starters include
massive fish salads and cold wild-cherry soup. After you've
washed a Gay Hussar three-courser down with, say, a bottle
of Bull's Blood, it's quite an achievement to stand up, never
mind return to work.

This is why it is a good idea to finish your meal with a reflective glass or two of Tokaji, Hungary's greatest wine, and one of the finest sweet wines in the world. Some call it the very finest.

It is made in the Tokaj region of northern Hungary, from the Furmint grape, which is packed with beguiling and subtle flavours that tend to emerge to best advantage in a sweet wine. Usually the grapes affected by botrytis, the noble rot, are picked first and the remainder turned into dry wine. The quality of the wine that emerges is defined by the number of hods of rotted, or *aszú*, grapes that go into the vat. Three *puttonyos* is the cheapest and least sweet, six the most stunning and the priciest.

During the Communist regime, Tokaji was grown for quantity rather than quality, and its extraordinary power and piercing flavour weakened. Now, however, it is back to the standard that made it a favourite in the Russian and Habsburg imperial courts. A glass of that, and your system can cope so much better with a Gay Hussar lunch.

After you've washed a Gay Hussar three-courser down with, say, a bottle of Bull's Blood, it's quite an achievement to stand up, never mind return to work.
This is why it is a good idea to finish your meal with a reflective glass or two of Tokay, Hungary's greatest wine

TORRES VIÑA SOL
Penedès, Spain
WHITE ○

Fresh 'n' fruity, crisp,
clean and unoaked

So, there I was in Beijing Capital International Airport with a rumbling stomach and a raging thirst. Inevitably, there was little choice in terms of where to eat: overpriced Asian-style dump or overpriced American-style dump. I chose the former.

Actually, the grub wasn't too bad at all – dim sum and a sloppy Thai curry of some sort – although the choice of drinks was hopeless. Except, hang on, didn't I see Torres Viña Sol on the list among the Fantas, Cokes, execrable Chinese wine and tasteless imported lager? I did, hooray, thank God for that! It was like bumping into an old mate at a wedding where I expected to know no-one. I all but flung my arms around the bottle and hugged it.

The Torres family has been making wine in Spain since 1870 (and more recently in Chile and California too) and – rather like Penfolds in Australia – is as rightly well-regarded for its entry-level wines, such as Viña Esmerelda, Sangre de Toro and said Viña Sol, as it is for its mid-range wines, such as Celeste, and its serious first-rate ones such as Grans Muralles, its fabled blend of indigenous Catalan varieties, and Mas La Plana, a finely-wrought, single vineyard, 100 per cent Cabernet Sauvignon which once famously beat a host of top clarets including Château Latour at a blind tasting in Paris. Jaime Torres, who founded the winery, spent much of his youth in Cuba and the Torres Milmanda Chardonnay was deemed sufficiently pukka to be served at the official banquet to welcome President Obama on his historic visit to Havana in 2016.

Viña Sol is a simple, fresh 'n' fruity, crisp, clean, unoaked, dry white wine made in Penedès from Parellada and you shouldn't expect to pay more than six quid a bottle for it retail. It's hugely dependable and jolly tasty with lots of crunchy apple and citrus flavours and I love it. I always breathe a contented sigh when I see any Torres wine on a restaurant list and it certainly warmed the cockles of my heart to see Viña Sol in Beijing.

VALPOLICELLA SUPERIORE
Veneto, Italy
RED ✪✪✪

Intense, rich
and rounded

I love Italian cooking, and believe that at the mid-range, bourgeois, unpretentious level it is actually better than French. Pappardelle with hare sauce, spicy sausages on a bed of luscious lentils, grilled chicken with herbs dotted in crispy skin – what is there not to like?

I can even stand the typical old-fashioned Italian restaurant in Britain, unchanged for decades, serving prosciutto and melon, glutinous osso buco, slabs of veal fried in breadcrumbs and served with a dollop of spaghetti and tomato sauce.

What is harder to forgive is some of the wine. Many of us have sorrowful memories of Valpolicella, a red wine from northern Italy, which has for long been a byword for dull and ordinary. For years the makers shovelled vast quantities of mediocre grapes into cooperative, industrial hoppers, producing a bland, dreary, predictable fluid, to be sold to people who had no idea how luscious Italian red wine could be.

But some Valpolicella Superiore can be. In the delectable examples made by Carlo Ferragù, a quantity of grapes – mostly Corvina, the best grown in the area – are put aside to dry before being added to the mix. They provide an extraordinarily intense flavour, rich and rounded, crowded with the taste of plums, damson, blackcurrants, to say nothing of vanilla and chocolate. It's a world away from the Valpol served at your local Casa Ordinario, and a delicious treat.

SERVING WINE

There is an awful lot of hoo-hah and pretension about serving wine. For instance, I detest those twee baskets that hold red wine at an angle. The theory is that any sediment will collect at what you might term 'the bottom of the bottom' of the bottle. The fact is that most red wines don't have a sediment, and if they do, the chances are that in the semi-darkness of a restaurant in the evening, or during a dinner party, you wouldn't even detect the telltale black lines when they appeared.

If you think red wine does have a sediment, then much the best thing is to decant it. A funnel makes life easier, but if you don't have one just pour more carefully. In either event pour slowly. You want to expose the wine to air. Put a piece of white paper on the table under the neck of the bottle and it should be easy to spot the grainy stuff when it starts to show. At that point, bring the bottle upright and stop.

Most people know that red wine is improved by contact with air – sometimes for several hours. (Though really old wines can go off very quickly. In Bordeaux, if they are drinking a wine that's been kept for decades, they will sometimes open the bottle and drink the contents immediately – even a few minutes can cause it to crumble like a vampire in daylight.)

What many people don't know is that white wines can improve just as much as red by getting a little exposure to the atmosphere. There are few things more disappointing than a really good white that has been kept in a fridge cold enough to keep milk and lettuce fresh, which is then thrust into an ice bucket to make it even colder. Low temperatures are fine for cheap white wines that have little flavour to start with and may have faults which it would be kind to mask with a blast of frigidity. But a good white wine will improve immeasurably if it is that bit warmer and has had a chance to breathe.

What many people don't know is that white wines can improve just as much as red by getting a little exposure to the atmosphere.

The rough rule is below 10°C for plonk, to above 12 for fine wines – many of which will go on releasing their flavours up to 16 degrees or so. (This doesn't apply to sweet whites, which should be drunk very cold – even the best – nor to a handful of whites, such as Chateau Musar, which the makers want you to serve at room temperature.)

I generally take a good white out of

the fridge about half an hour before serving, and keep it in one of those twin-walled bucket affairs that act as double glazing. They don't cool the wine, but they keep it at the right temperature for much longer. They're especially useful if you're drinking white or rosé wine at a picnic on a hot day.

What is vital is to stop the stuff tasting like boiled soup, an unwanted result you can easily achieve by leaving the bottle on the radiator. I have seen bottles made to stand on an Aga, which in its way is as cruel as doing it to your cat.

In fact, a good white wine is improved by being decanted, just as much as a good red. The problem is that the result looks a little like a hospital sample. If you don't want to decant it, pour small portions for everyone, and encourage them to warm the wine with their hands and swill it round in the glass so that the air gets to it. If you have a bottle that needs chilling in a hurry, you can put it briefly in the freezer compartment. Some people claim that the sudden chill strips the flavour away. I haven't found that, though I wouldn't risk it with a superb Burgundy, for instance. Of course you must remember to take it out after, say, 15 minutes or there is a danger of the wine freezing and expanding, making the bottle explode.

I also keep one or two of those silvery jackets filled with gel in the freezer. Slip this over a warm white bottle and it should be drinkable in five or ten minutes. (The jacket doesn't chill the neck, so I pour one, still warmish, glass and put it to one side. Then serve the stuff from the body of the bottle, replace the first lot, and pop what's left in the fridge.)

Red wines are generally served at room temperature, though that rule was laid down in the days before central heating when houses were colder. Now we like to keep our living quarters at 20 degrees or more, reds can be a little too warm. Cellar temperature might be better. What is vital is to stop the stuff tasting like boiled soup, an unwanted result you can easily achieve by leaving the bottle on the radiator. I have seen bottles made to stand on an Aga, which in its way is as cruel as doing it to your cat. The result is ghastly. A little bit colder than the ambient temperature is about right in most cases. And some reds are better off cool. Red Loire wines, for example, or the cheaper Beaujolais. Half an hour in the fridge, or outside the back door in winter, should be adequate.

One problem people often face is keeping wine that's been opened but not finished. With whites it is not a problem. Just pop a cork, or a rubber cork substitute, into the neck and keep it in the fridge. What most people don't realize is that you can do exactly the same with red wine. Just take it out an hour or so before you propose to start on the bottle again. I wouldn't recommend this with really top-rate wines, but for most everyday bottles it works perfectly well.

Alternatives include the Vacu-Vin™, a rubber stopper with a slit in the top. A hand-operated plastic pump draws air out through the slit which is sealed tight by the outside pressure. In theory, it leaves a vacuum in the bottle. It may be my imagination – though I don't think it is – but a lot of the flavour of the wine is sucked out with the air. What you have next day is drinkable, well preserved, but rather dull. A better alternative is a can of nitrogen, sold in many specialist wine and cookery stores. You spray a few quick bursts into the bottle, and the gas – safe and flavour-free – settles on the surface of the wine. Some experts reckon it will keep red wine in good shape for as long as a week.

When we say wine is 'corked' we don't mean that it has bits of cork floating on the top – that may be mildly annoying but has no effect on the taste – but that the cork and then the wine has been tainted by a compound known as TCA, created by airborne fungi.

A corked wine can taste so slightly musty that only a real expert can detect that it's off, or it might taste of vinegar. Some estimates suggest that one bottle in 20 may be corked, though often people don't trust their own judgement enough to be sure. Absolutely any reputable wine merchant or supermarket will replace a corked bottle, though you need

to get it back to the store sharpish along with your receipt. They're not going to replace something that's gone bad because you've had it lying around the house for a month.

The argument rages about screwcaps, or 'Stelvin closures' as they are technically known. Certainly they reduce hugely the number of bad wines. (I have had a foul bottle with a screwcap, but it was probably due to a fault in the manufacture of the wine.) Some people suggest that the tiny amount of air admitted by even a good cork actually helps a fine wine to mature, and this might be so – it's almost impossible to tell. Others don't want to lose the mystique of drawing the cork and the pleasing 'pop' that results. (A cartoon in the Circle of Wine Writers newsletter showed a mediaeval commercial traveller showing a tavern-keeper a new-fangled invention, the glass bottle. 'No,' says the barman. 'My customers will always prefer the romance of goatskin.')

The cork should emerge with a gentle susurration reminiscent, as somebody once remarked, of a duchess farting.

Years ago I went to a tasting of vintage ports, and the oldest was from 1900. I was struck by how many were perfectly preserved and even the most ancient tasted good, if a little faded. I asked the maker what kind of closure he would like, and

he groaned gently. He was legally obliged to use cork because the cork industry is so important to Portugal. But, he said, his ideal would be a crown, the rubber or cork-lined cap with crinkly edges familiar from beer bottles. But the day when your waiter produces a bottle opener and flips the top off your Meursault 2003 is, I think, still some way off.

With champagne, and most other sparkling wines, hold the cork firmly, then use your other hand to twist the bottle slowly and gently. The cork should emerge with a gentle susurration reminiscent, as somebody once remarked, of a duchess farting. Occasionally some of the wine will foam out anyway, so keep a glass handy. Normally, however, all you will see is a light, curly wisp from the top of the bottle, and it is ready to pour.

In the unusual event of your having an unfinished bottle of bubbly, close it with an ordinary cork (you'll never get the original cork back), but not too tight, so that if pressure builds up the thing won't fire out of the bottle like a cannonball. Don't bother putting a teaspoon upside down in the neck to preserve the bubbles – that's a myth. In fact, for 24 hours or so it should remain pleasantly frothy. Often the reduced amount of carbon dioxide, plus the exposure to air, means that the champagne tastes even better than it did when it was first opened. Indeed, the test of a great champagne is its flavour after it's gone flat.

TINTO «VALBUENA» 5º
Ribera del Duero

Savoury and
lip-smacking

VEGA SICILIA
Ribera del Duero, Spain
RED ✪✪✪✪✪

The late disc jockey John Peel could never quite remember the name of the wine he liked. 'Let's have some of that one with the "J" in it,' he'd say to his producer when they went to the wine bar. Indeed Rioja was enormously popular in Britain at the time. It still is. But it isn't really as good as a wine from a neighbouring region that has been well known for only a couple of decades.

Probably the best single wine region in the whole of Spain these days is Ribera del Duero. The Duero River flows west into Portugal, where it is called the Douro and is the home of port, plus many other delectable wines. In Spain they make wonderfully powerful wines, savoury and lip-smacking. And the best of the lot is probably Vega Sicilia, which has nothing to do with Sicily, but derives from the original estate where it is made, the Pago de la Vega Santa Cecilia y Carrascal. So it really just means Cecilia's field.

The wine was originally made in small quantities, given away to friends of the owners. Ironically it won two prizes at the Barcelona World's Fair of 1929, yet because the region was not a *denominación de origen*, the Spanish version of *appellation controlée*, it could only be sold as table wine. Which did not prevent the cognoscenti from acquiring it.

Then, in 1982, the area did get DO status, and Ribera del Duero began to take off around the world. At Vega Sicilia, they keep up their flagship reputation by the most meticulous care. Grapes (mainly a local version of Tempranillo) are harvested – by hand – as late as possible to make sure they have the maximum-possible flavour. They are sorted in the shed and many are rejected. Then the wine is matured for ten years before it goes on sale. They make only 25,000 cases, and while 300,000 bottles may seem a lot, it is a droplet in the wine lake. Some 2,000 people are on a waiting list for allocations. You might be better off trying to get a Manchester United season ticket.

VERNACCIA DI SAN GIMIGNANO
Tuscany, Italy
WHITE ✪

Very drinkable, leafy and citric

The great towers of San Gimignano are among the finest sights in Tuscany. They were built by wealthy merchants to show off; the taller your tower, the richer – and so more important – you were. Freud would have little trouble interpreting that. When I first went there, decades ago, the place was popular but still accessible; there were plenty of tourists, to be sure, but not so many that the place resembled a Central Line train in rush hour. Towards the evening, as the sun set on the towers, and the visitors began to leave, it took on a lustrous yet ghostly quality. If you sat in a café with a glass of the local wine, you could imagine you were in a catacomb, or trapped in a coral reef, lost in a ghost city like a half-remembered Doré engraving.

It is much more crowded now. You have to leave your car in one of the large parking lots outside the city gates. This is obviously practical, but increases the sense that you are merely undergoing some kind of tourist experience, ticking a box on your travels. San Gimignano, it seems to me, has lost that dreamlike quality and will perhaps never regain it.

But the wine is still good. It is not a great white wine, but it is very drinkable, leafy and citric, and it's a nice glass to cool you off on an Italian summer day. But it does travel, too, and is good with lots of foods, not only Italian. The name is somewhat confusing, since there are grapes called *vernaccia* all over Italy. It comes from the word *vernaculo*, meaning 'local' or 'indigenous', and is a completely different kettle of fish from other *vernaccia* in the rest of the country, some of which are actually red.

VILLA WOLF PINOT GRIS
Pfalz, Germany
WHITE ✪—✪✪

It's a wine that can be drunk with almost any food, and yet is quite capable of being enjoyed as an apéritif

Gosh, Doctor Loosen makes lovely wines. His Pinot Gris is so good that even though I once saw it on a restaurant wine list at four times its regular retail price, I decided to have it anyway. But how much better to buy four bottles in an off-licence and drink them at home!

It's a very unusual wine, too. For one thing, not much Pinot Gris is made in Germany. When it is, it's normally sold under its German name, *grauburgunder*, or 'grey Burgundy', which doesn't sound like a lot of fun. This is made in the Pfalz, the German region just north of Alsace, where much Pinot Gris is also produced. In the 19th century, the estate was a hugely successful vineyard owned by Johann Ludwig Wolf, who made enough money from it to erect a grand Italianate mansion on the property.

It is now owned by Dr Ernst Loosen, who decided to start experimenting. He felt that the Pinot Gris that was slopping around the world – chiefly cheap Italian sold as Pinot Grigio – was thin, watery and generally not up to snuff. The variety, after all, can make a zestful and fragrant wine; what was the point in using it to create something close to alcoholic washing-up water? By contrast, he found the Pinot Gris in neighbouring Alsace too thick and heavy for his taste. So he set out to find a middle course, and succeeded triumphantly.

It's a wine that can be drunk with almost any food, and yet is quite capable of being enjoyed as an apéritif. (Note for anoraks who care about these things: half the wine is fermented in oak barrels to give it complexity, and the other half in stainless steel to preserve its fruity zing. A wine Goldilocks would have enjoyed.)

Dr Loosen, who keeps picking up awards for his winemaking from all over the place, also makes a dry Riesling which is perfectly attuned to British tastes, being bone-dry but with a nice floral flavour. His 2007, a great year in Germany, is particularly good.

Half the wine is fermented in oak barrels
to give it complexity, and the other half
in stainless steel to preserve its fruity zing.
A wine Goldilocks would have enjoyed.

Deeply pungent flavour, honeyed, nutty and spicy, often with that undertone of curry

VIN JAUNE
Jura, France

YELLOW WINE ✪✪✪

Vin Jaune is one of the world's more extraordinary wines. The way it is made bears some resemblance to sherry, though the end result is very different: rich, and spicy. It is one of the few wines you'll find where remarking on the taste of curry is regarded as a compliment to the maker.

It comes from the smallest wine region in France, the Jura, in the far east, sandwiched between Burgundy and Switzerland. The making of Vin Jaune is utterly bound and trussed up by tradition. The grapes have to be local Savagnin. These are picked late – sometimes as late as December – when they are at their very ripest. After being fermented they are left in old Burgundy barrels, which are put in attics, cellars, or wherever there will be substantial variations in the temperature. This is important. A third or more of the wine evaporates. Naturally air gets to what is left, but that doesn't matter because by this time, it has grown a film of yeast which preserves the wine as it ages. A similar film, *flor*, is used in making sherry.

All the time the wine is in barrels, it is tested to make sure it isn't going off the rails. Then, after six years and three months, it is bottled in the local flask, a *clavelin* of 62 centilitres. This is traditionally the proportion of an original litre that is left. Some leading producers will reject as much as three-quarters of the wine and sell it off simply as Savagnin blanc.

The good stuff is remarkable, having a deeply pungent flavour, honeyed, nutty and spicy, often with that curry undertone. You might even try it with a tandoori, though curry houses are not exactly common in the Jura. Instead, locals enjoy it with a roasted free-range chicken, or cheese and walnuts. The best Vin Jaune can last as long as 50 years.

It is made all over the Jura, though the finest comes from the village of Château-Chalon. It is the only Vin Jaune that does not say 'Vin Jaune' on the label. This seems perverse, though possibly it is designed to stop foreigners spotting it and carting off car-boot-loads.

VIOGNIER
WHITE ○○—○○○○

The finest Viognier comes from Condrieu, a tiny region of the northern Rhône (see page 43). But it is now so popular that it's grown all over the world. It is not an easy grape to handle. Catch it too early, and it will have none of the lovely, evanescent, luscious, perfumed, ripe stone-fruit flavours that its fans adore so much. It needs to be grown in small quantities, otherwise quality vanishes. It is also one of the few high-class whites that need to be drunk young; leave even the best more than a year or two in bottle, and you'll have something dull and sludgy.

A good Viognier is a prize in any cellar

But a good Viognier is a prize in any cellar (or, at least, kitchen; you cannot leave it and forget it). That is what Josh Jensen, a Clint Eastwood lookalike, thought when he visited Condrieu in the 1960s, was bowled over by the joys of this almost unknown grape, and took cuttings back home to California, where he still produces some of the finest New World bottles. In 1965, there were only eight hectares grown in Condrieu and one year they produced a mere 1,900 litres. But a quarter of a century later this had risen to 80 hectares and this is still increasing.

Meanwhile, other winemakers around the world had started producing the grape. As always, you get what you pay for, but there are some excellent *vins de pays* in southern France, some first-rate Viogniers in Australia, and now many wineries in the States, including an up-and-coming region, Virginia. But Viognier vines need to be at least 15 years old to produce the best wines, and it's a joy to know that, for this reason, worldwide quality is going to rise year after year.

WARWICK ESTATE PROFESSOR BLACK SAUVIGNON BLANC

Stellenbosch, South Africa

WHITE ○○

Undertones of lemons, pears, limes, grapefruit, figs, basil, aniseed

This really is a terrific Sauvignon Blanc, packed with flavour, bringing undertones of lemons, pears, limes, grapefruit, figs, basil, aniseed – and, according to some, 'dusty talc' and 'candy floss', neither of which would seem like much of a selling point. That's wine writers for you. They take pride in putting you off. But it is absolutely first-rate, being pure and fresh and totally refreshing. The grapes are harvested at different times to get the maximum flavours and, like many of the best wines, it's left on its own lees for a few months, just to cram more flavour into the bottle. Scrumptious. It should be good, too, coming from Warwick Estate, one of the finest and most highly esteemed wineries in South Africa.

The land was bought after the Boer War by Col. Alexander Gordon, who named it after his regiment, the Warwickshires. In those days they grew various other crops, but in 1964 vines were planted. Professor Malcolm Black had nothing to do with wine. He was a fruit specialist at the University of Stellenbosch, who had been given the job of developing an early-ripening peach to get ahead of the market. This he duly did, but when peach prices dropped, the new owners pulled up the trees on his patch of land and planted Sauvignon Blanc – and, to the great delight of the professor's widow, named it after him. She was an opera singer, and it's not ridiculously fanciful to say that the wine is reminiscent of a soprano's top note, being clear and resonant.

WICKHAM SPECIAL RELEASE FUMÉ

Hampshire, England

WHITE ○

I was sitting next to a French winemaker some years ago in a French château and I made the mistake of praising English wine. He gave me one of those looks the French do so well: not rude, but not exactly courteous, either, conveying disdainful bafflement anyone could be so misguided. 'Yurr English wine,' he said, 'eet tastes of rain.'

Well, in those days a lot of it did. But very few English vineyards would dream of offering something pluvially flavoured now. Instead they can produce wines that would hold their own in any company, often at prices which match, or improve on, those in the rest of the world. If the pound sterling remains low, that will be very important over the next few years.

Wickham Fumé is another wine that made a very popular choice on the House of Commons wine list. In 2008 this 'Special Release' won the prize for best English wine aged in oak, and it's easy to see why. Made from a blend of the white Bacchus and Reichensteiner grapes, it is perfectly suited to English conditions, and aged in French oak, it becomes a wine of great depth, sold at a very reasonable price. The vineyard is just outside Southampton, and like many English winemakers the Wickham people have made it quite a tourist centre: there are tours, tastings, a shop and rather a good restaurant.

Perfectly suited to English conditions, and aged in French oak, it becomes a wine of great depth, sold at a very reasonable price

DOMAINE ZIND-HUMBRECHT GEWURZTRAMINER
Alsace, France
WHITE ✪✪–✪✪✪

A stunning brew with a powerful flavour

Léonard and Olivier Humbrecht, the father and son who make these wines, are an intriguing pair. For one thing Olivier was the first French person to become a Master of Wine. This is the prestigious title that allows someone who has passed the exams to put the letters MW after his or her name. Even now, there are fewer than 300 MWs, two-thirds of them British and only just over a dozen of them French. There is probably as much work involved in getting the precious letters as there is in a tough degree course in a science subject; you have to know the stuff and you cannot just wing it. Which is why leading merchants often give their most promising staff plenty of time off to do the course. The qualification doesn't just help anyone who has it to progress in the trade; it adds lustre to whomever he or she works for.

They need it. Becoming an MW requires a literally encyclopaedic knowledge of how wine is made, where it is made, what it is made from, the techniques by which it is made, the bugs and diseases that afflict it, the way it is marketed, the traditions and the history – the list is literally endless. You could start by reading Jancis Robinson's *Oxford Companion to Wine*. If you committed its 815 pages and 3,000 entries to memory, you'd be halfway there. Then there's the practical test, which consists of three blind tastings, each of a dozen wines. It might be 12 from the same winery, which you have to place in order of vintage; or 12 Cabernet Sauvignons from 12 countries; or a dozen whites from different grapes, each of which you have to identify.

All of which merely shows that Olivier Humbrecht knows an awful lot about wine. He and his father (his mother was Geneviève Zind, hence the double-barrelled name of the company) are obsessional about producing superb Alsace wines. They have several properties in the region, totalling only 30 hectares. Since they make only 35 hectolitres per

hectare, compared to the legally permissible 70 hectolitres, they are able to keep standards incredibly high.

They also bought up prime sites on steep slopes which other growers didn't want to use because they can't be worked by machines. They also – and here I'm afraid they begin to lose me – make their wine biodynamically, according to the phases of the moon, and bury cow horns in the soil to improve its vitality.

Nobody claims to have detected the flavour of cow horn in the bottle, but the end result is a series of wines, chiefly Riesling, Pinot Gris and Gewurztraminer, which are as good as any in Alsace and in some people's opinion, better. Their Gewurz is a stunning brew. To list the flavours some say they've found there – lychees, apples, clotted cream, oranges, white pepper, smoke and sea salt – is to ignore the sheer power of the finished product. It wallops you. Irrelevant to ponder which food it would go with; the wine is a force of nature and you should probably drink it on its own. Some people don't actually like it; they feel it is all much too much. The best vintages will last for 15-20 years. It is not cheap, but for such incredible quality, it is sensational value.

HOW TO FIND THE WINES MENTIONED IN THIS BOOK

This shouldn't usually be too difficult, except in the case of some of the more obscure bottles. Many of the wines I've described are generic: for example, you can find Claret, Burgundy, Beaujolais, even German wines, pretty well anywhere, though I have listed suppliers where I've specified a particular wine as being especially good.

The problems start when vineyards and producers start to shift their suppliers. Nothing is carved in the rock; a grower might decide he can get a better price elsewhere and move to a different merchant. Or the same merchant might buy stocks of a wine with great enthusiasm, only to find that it doesn't sell, and drop it from the list.

Luckily, in this electronic age it should be easy to find almost any wine by means of one of the internet sites that will root out bottles for you.

Among the best are:

www.cellartracker.com
www.wine-searcher.com
www.bordeauxindex.com
www.decanter.com/winefinder, run by Britain's leading wine magazine

RECOMMENDED WINE MERCHANTS IN THE UK

Adnams
adnams.co.uk

Avery's of Bristol
averys.com

Berry Bros & Rudd
bbr.com

Corney & Barrow
corneyandbarrow.com

D. Byrne & Co
dbyrne-finewines.co.uk

El Vino
elvino.co.uk

Fortnum & Mason
fortnumandmason.com

FromVineyardsDirect
fromvineyardsdirect.com

Graham Mitchell
gcmv.co.uk

Hedley Wright
hedleywright.com

Lea & Sandeman
leaandsandeman.co.uk

Luvians Bottle Shop
luvians.com

Majestic
majestic.co.uk

Philglas & Swiggott
philglas-swiggot.com

Private Cellar
privatecellar.co.uk

Roberson Wine
robersonwine.com

Stone, Vine & Sun
stonevine.co.uk

Swig
swig.co.uk

Tanners Wines
tanners-wines.co.uk

Vintage Roots
vintageroots.co.uk

Waddesdon Manor
waddesdononlineshop.org

The Wine Company
thewinecompany.co.uk

The Wine Society
thewinesociety.com

Wrightson Wines
wrightsonwines.co.uk

Yapp Bros
yapp.co.uk

INDEX

ACKNOWLEDGEMENTS

The publisher would like to thank the following for their help in providing labels and information:
p15 castromartin.com; p22 armit.co.uk; p24 domaine-andre-colonge-et-fils.com; p26 Bishops
Head Wines/privatecellar.co.uk; p26 bodegasborsao.com; p27, p92, p130, p138 yapp.co.uk; p28
songlinesestates.com; p29 adnams.co.uk; p31 Domain Daniel Dampt; p32 Ponnaz et fils, winemaker
at Cully; p40, p53, p170 Berry Bros & Rudd (bbr.com); p41 Patricia Atkinson patricia.atkinson@
wanadoo.frl; p42 ©Jean-Luc Colombo/Hatch Mansfield; p55 John Duval Wines john_duval@
bigpond.com; p56 bob@camelvalley.com; p59 liviofelluga.it; p67 fells.co.uk; p72, p87, p127
corneyandbarrow.com; p75 hegartychamans.com; p80 jacksonestate.co.nz; p82 monteswines.com;
p93 mitchellwines.com; p105 hedleywright.demon.co.uk; p106 taltarni.com.au; p107 Vignobles Perse;
p110 pesqueraafernandez.com; p118 Joseph Phelps Vineyards jpvwines.com; p120 axamillesimes.
com; p122 beyerskloof.co.za; p126 © Valdo Spumanti; p133 Rustenberg Wines rustenberg.co.za;
p136 stonevine.co.uk; p142 Vignoble de la Coulée de Serrant coulee-de-serrant.com; p145
Manzanilla Papirusi Sherry ©Fields, Morris & Verdin (BBR group); p146, p147, p157 swig.co.uk;
p148 chateaudesours.com; p149 Spy Valley Wines spyvalley.co.nz; p150 timadamswines.com.au;
p153 antinori.it; p164 drloosen.com,jlwolf.com; p166 chateauchalon.com; p167 renwood.com;
p169 Wickham Vineyard wineshare.co.uk

Editorial director Sarah Lavelle
Creative director Helen Lewis
Senior editor Céline Hughes
Designer Nicola Ellis
Design assistant Gemma Hayden
Illustrator Claudio Muñoz
Production manager Stephen Lang
Production director Vincent Smith

First published in 2009 by
Quadrille Publishing Limited

This updated edition published in 2016
Pentagon House
52–54 Southwark Street
London SE1 1UN
www.quadrille.co.uk

Quadrille is an imprint of Hardie Grant
www.hardiegrant.com.au

Cataloguing in Publication Data: A catalogue record
for this book is available from the British Library.

ISBN 978 184949 892 0

Printed and bound in China